CW01626698

Pelagia, Edward, Anne and Delphine Garland are all dancers and ballet mad. Their mother is a prima ballerina and their father a conductor of the ballet company orchestra.

When their cousin Joan is orphaned she comes down from Lancashire to live with the Garlands in London. Confused and lonely, Joan finds it hard to fit in, especially as her cousins are rather wary of her and don't understand how Joan could survive without knowing anything about ballet!

But Joan does survive and begins to enjoy her new life observing the ups and downs and tears and triumphs of her glamorous cousins.

By the same author:

The Ballet Family Again
The Ballet Twins
Ballet for Drina
Drina's Dancing Year
Drina Dances in Exile
Drina Dances in Italy
Drina Dances Again
Drina Dances in New York

The Ballet Family

by

Jean Estoril

Macdonald Children's Books

Cover illustration by Anne Eggebert
Black and white illustrations by Beryl Sanders

A MACDONALD BOOK

Text copyright © Mabel Esther Allan 1963
Illustrations copyright © Macdonald Children's Books 1989

First published in Great Britain by
Methuen & Co Ltd

This edition published in 1989 by
Macdonald Children's Books

All characters in the publication are fictitious, and any resemblance to real persons, living or dead, is purely coincidental.

All rights reserved

This book is sold subject to the condition that it shall not, by way of trade or otherwise, be lent, re-sold, hired out, or otherwise circulated without the publishers' prior consent in any form of binding or cover other than that in which it is published and without a similar condition including this condition being imposed on the subsequent purchaser.

Photoset in North Wales by
Derek Doyle & Associates, Mold, Clwyd

Printed and bound in Great Britain at
The Guernsey Press

Macdonald Children's Books
Simon and Schuster International group
Wolsey House, Wolsey Road
Hemel Hempstead HP2 4SS

BRITISH LIBRARY CATALOGUING IN PUBLICATION DATA
Estoril, Jean, *1915-*
The ballet family.
Rn: Mabel Esther Allan I. Title
823'.914[J]

ISBN 0-356-16796-8
ISBN 0-356-16797-6 Pbk

Contents

Chapter One
The Garlands

The early September sun was streaming into the studio at the top of the tall, thin house in Moone Crescent. From where she stood by the window Delphine, the youngest of the four Garlands, could see the lake in Regent's Park, surrounded by trees and reflecting the blue sky.

The record came to an end and the older boy and girl who were practising at the *barre* fixed to the longest wall did one or two more *pliés* in the second position.

"Stick it back to the beginning!" said Edward at last. "Thought you were in charge of the record-player, Delph?"

There was no answer. Delphine's thin, straight back remained turned to them.

"Delph!"

"Oh, shut up! I'm thinking."

"I'll do it." Anne ran across to the record-player. She was thirteen, more than three years older than Delphine, and she looked very slim in her green leotard. The bright colour suited her well, for every one of the Garland children had their mother's red hair, and Anne's was, as people sometimes said, redder than most.

"Why don't you go out, Delph?" she asked, as she bent

over the record. "Take Bonne for a run by the lake. Or else come and practise."

Delphine turned then, pushing back her tumbled curls with a restless, disgruntled gesture.

"I took Bonne out before breakfast and what's the *good* of practising? It's just a waste of time; I decided that definitely last night. I shall never be a dancer. I shall be the family tragedy; the skeleton in the cupboard. People will say – they're probably saying it already – 'Oh, poor little Delphine! Just no good at all. And fancy! When her mother is *prima ballerina* of the Thorburg Company and her sister is the most prominent member of the *corps de ballet*'."

"Pelagia isn't. Not the most promising, I mean. She's the youngest member of the *corps* and who can tell?" Anne squatted by the record-player, while Edward, who was fourteen and looked older, strolled forward.

"Stop agonizing, you young idiot. We've had two months of it. And you may as well practise, for you know jolly well that you won't give up dancing. You've scarcely started and you'll get to the Thorburg School in the end."

Delphine flopped down in a patch of sunlight, then arranged herself in an attitude of conscious grace.

"You look like a sylphide with a headache!" said Anne.

She was deeply sorry for Delphine, who had certainly had her troubles and humiliations lately, but she was always so self-conscious. She never just sat; she struck an attitude.

"I've got a heartache," said Delphine dolefully. "My heart has felt like a stone since that audition in July. It *was* a tragedy; you know it was. You all just took it for granted that I'd be accepted."

"I suppose we did," Anne admitted. "I did, anyway, and *you* certainly did. I suppose that was part of the trouble, only you don't like it if anyone says so. You went off so cockily, and you said yourself that you didn't take it as seriously as you should have done. You thought that just because Mother is a ballerina, and Father conducts the orchestra, Mr Thorburg and the company ballet mistress and everyone would fall on your neck and say: 'Ah, the most promising Garland of the lot!' But it was hard – it was awful. Only there were lots of good reasons for it. There were only twenty places for this term and over seventy applicants, and you *were* only nine then and you know quite well that they all explained to Father and Mother that they thought you'd do better just to stay at your ordinary school for a while and go on learning from Madame Darinova."

"And that being so," said Edward, "you should be practising with us, or at any rate not mooning about, moaning."

"I tell you I'm giving up all thought of being a dancer. I might be an actress instead. I have looks and personality –"

"You're insufferably conceited at times. Come off it!"

"I hate you, Edward!" But Delphine said it without heat. "Anyway, I've really quite decided, and I wouldn't go to the Thorburg School now if they paid me. The iron has eaten into my soul during these last two months."

"It's rapidly eating into mine. Stick that record on again, Bunchy."

Anne paused with the arm of the record-player in her hand.

"You know I said that I wouldn't be called Bunchy any more. It's silly. I'm the least bunchy of girls. Too thin, if anything."

"It'll stick, though. What can you expect when you're A. Garland? Let's get on. We were late starting."

Far down in the house the front door bell shrilled.

"Oh, do go and answer it, Delph. Annali's out shopping and Rosa's probably in the garden trying to find some flowers for the house."

"Oh, of course it has to be me!"

The bell rang again and the sad sylphide rose from the floor, smoothing her yellow cotton dress.

"I bet it's only someone selling."

But a few minutes later she came back with two tickets in her hand. Her brother and sister left the *barre* and the record played on unheeded.

"It was Mrs Jolly. They can't go to Covent Garden this evening and they wonder if we can use their tickets. Stalls Circle."

"Oh, I say! What luck!" Anne cried. She loved the Royal Opera House perhaps even more than the smaller Thorburg Theatre at the top of Kingsway. "It's *Giselle* and –"

"Father and Mother can't go," said Edward. "They're both on tonight and so is Pelagia."

"If anyone goes it ought to be me! I went down," Delphine cried shrilly.

Anne frowned. They had been to the Opera House alone, of course, but always on Saturday afternoons and usually in the amphitheatre. But it was unlikely that the tickets would be wasted.

"I suppose we'd better toss up. That's the fairest."

"I always lose. You know I do. And you've seen *Giselle* at least forty-nine times. I've only seen it twice. It's ages since it was in the Thorburg repertoire."

"And I expect I'll see it another forty-nine, but I'll never tire of it. Anyway, leave it till later. We *must* get on. It's a shame to be indoors."

The record stopped and they heard the telephone ringing below. Edward groaned, Anne rolled her eyes in despair and Delphine flopped back into her sylphide attitude on the floor.

"I'm not going down again. Yell to Rosa out of one of the back windows. She's the one who moons, thinking about Switzerland."

Anne gave a resigned sigh and ran down to answer the

insistent bell. After a few minutes they heard her calling and both went to lean over the white painted banisters. She was standing on the landing below, rumpling her hair and looking worried.

"I hope I did the right thing. I know how Father hates to be called out of a full rehearsal. But I had to give the theatre number, as it seems so serious."

"What was it?"

"Someone from the North. Rochdale. Quite a Lancashire voice she had and she sounded so upset. Father's sister died very suddenly this morning. She kept on talking about 'poor Joan'. That's our cousin, isn't it?"

Edward, too, looked worried.

"Yes, you know it is."

"She's always seemed so remote, as though she lives in darkest Africa. Her father's dead, isn't he, so she must be quite alone. I hope they get hold of Father."

"He'll probably have to go up to Rochdale, but he can't until after the performance tonight. Look here! It's hopeless to practise this morning. There are too many interruptions. We'd better change and go out."

Anne nodded and whisked into the room that she shared with Pelagia. Pulling off her leotard and reaching for a thin cotton dress she continued to frown, thinking of the cousin she had never met. She knew that her aunt had married a schoolmaster from the North, at the same time giving up a promising career as a concert pianist; and when her husband died she had continued to live in Lancashire. She had insisted that she was happy there, disliked London and would be entirely out of things now in her brother's world.

Joan Bradshaw must be at least thirteen, Anne thought, as she ran downstairs calling to Bonne-Bouche, their black poodle. It must be dreadful to have your mother die and to be quite alone, or only with a rather hysterical woman with a Lancashire voice.

Edward joined her as she was putting on the dog's lead.

"The morning's simply flown and we've done nothing. We haven't time to go far."

"No, but we may as well take Bonne for a run before lunch. Where's Delph?"

"*I* don't know. In her present mood she's better left alone."

They stepped out into the elegant little crescent where most of the houses were charmingly painted, with wrought-iron balconies, colourful window-boxes and bushes in bright tubs by the front doors.

The poodle capered cheerfully on the end of his long red lead as they crossed the busy Outer Circle and entered the park, and Anne drew a breath of relief. It was good to be out and to put the slightly unsatisfactory events of the morning behind them. But *could* they put them behind them? There was still the unknown Joan, motherless in Rochdale.

"I wonder what Rochdale's like?" she said musingly, as they approached the lake, picking their way through playing children. On this fine Saturday the park was crowded.

"Pretty grim, I should imagine. All that part is. Cotton mills, and people wearing clogs and shawls, and – and bleak hills."

Anne shivered, looking lovingly at the familiar London scene.

"How dreadful! I'd hate to live anywhere but London. But do you really think that people still wear shawls and clogs? And I don't think there are cotton mills now."

"No, probably not. High heels and ordinary clothes. Lots of headscarves; I've seen 'em on television. But it still sounds grim."

"Aunt Peggy liked it, though. Father once said she was sunk in it; he couldn't understand how. I wonder if he *will* go?"

"Bound to, I should think. Someone's got to rescue the poor kid."

"And bring her to London?"

"I don't know. I suppose so."

"Oh, I do really hope not. We're so – so compact and right. What should we do with a cousin from Rochdale? I feel awfully sorry for her, but I must admit I don't want her."

"Small choice we'll have, I expect," said Edward.

He turned out to be right. When they returned they found the car at the door and their father and mother in the living-room, arguing over a timetable.

"It'll have to be a sleeper on the midnight train to Manchester," Mr Garland was saying, frowning at the small print. "If I wait till tomorrow it will mean Sunday trains and we know what those are like. I'll ring up and try and book. Luckily I can stay on there until Tuesday. Mrs Thwaite said the funeral was to be early Tuesday morning. But I must be back for *Coppélia* at night. Fortunately Wertzer's conducting on Monday."

"Father's going to bring Cousin Joan to live here!" Delphine cried from the sofa.

"What else can he do?" Mona Garland asked. She was thirty-nine, but with her soft red hair, clear complexion and slim figure looked many years younger. "That poor child! She must have had a terrible time. She can have the little guest room by the studio. It's the best we can do and I'm afraid it will mean no more visitors. Annali will make it extra nice for her."

"Poor Peggy," said Mr Garland. "It seems she'd been ill for quite a time, but no one thought it was very serious. Then last night she was taken to hospital and she died at nine this morning. I wish now that I'd kept more in touch with her. I haven't seen her since that time I met her in Manchester."

"Well, it's no use being sorry. She quite definitely cut herself off. I think she always felt rather impatient with what she called 'our ballet world'. She was very musical, I know, but she just didn't care for the ballet."

Just then Annali, their elderly Swiss cook-housekeeper, who had been with the family for nearly twenty years, announced that lunch was ready, and Pelagia arrived breathlessly as they took their places.

"I had to stay behind to try on a costume. They told me you'd gone and about the telephone call." She would be eighteen in November and was very like her mother, except that she wore her straight red hair caught back smoothly in a knot, a style much favoured by the members of the *corps de ballet*.

"There's another thing," said Edwin Garland, when they had reached the meat course. "Perhaps it's hardly the time to talk about it, but as it's good news – I had a word with Thorburg before the rehearsal, Delph. You'll be pleased to know that they're letting you into school this month after all."

Delphine shot upright, waving her fork.

"How do you mean? They turned me down. I – I wouldn't go now for all the gold in the world."

Her father looked at her rather sternly. In many ways he was a very quiet man and, though he would never have admitted it, Delphine was his favourite, but her manner, not to say manners, had left much to be desired lately.

"Of course you would. In fact, we've both agreed. In the light of everything that's happened since July we think it would be best. Two of the girls who were accepted at the audition aren't taking up their places, after all, and you minded so much being refused that –"

"Of course I minded, Father. It was a dire insult."

"It wasn't meant as such. At the time they thought it

might be best to wait a little. But we've all talked a good deal about it since then, and with these two sisters going to Canada unexpectedly – well, you get your place; so you can tell Madame. And I hope you work well."

Delphine glared as fiercely as she dared.

"They don't really want me. It's just to please you and Mother."

"Not really. We didn't argue over the original decision. But now you've got what you wanted, and on Monday you'll have to get your uniform. And that'll be the last Garland to enter the Thorburg School."

"I won't go! Why should I? Can't I try for the Royal Ballet School instead?"

"Don't be silly, Delphine," her mother said quietly. "You know the Thorburg's the only place for you. With Edward and Anne already there –"

"That's just it. I've thought about it and decided that, if I must dance, I'd sooner strike out on my own. But really I'd sooner go to a Stage School. There are too many Garlands in this dancing racket –"

The rest of the family burst out laughing.

"There are rather a number," agreed Pelagia. "But one more won't make much difference. Accept and be thankful, Delphine."

"*Must* I?"

"I've told you we've already made up our minds."

"I shall hate it. My – my attitude has changed. If they'd taken me when they had the chance –"

"They've taken you now, so let's hear no more about it. I must go and telephone before I have my pudding." And Edwin Garland rose and walked out into the hall.

Delphine sank back, muttering: "Cousins from Rochdale and condescension from the Thorburg School. Now they'll kindly give me a chance. I hate them!"

"Oh, don't be a cuckoo, Delph!"

"It's true. They didn't think me any good. I'm a failure. Well, I shall enjoy being one."

The eyes of the rest met in half-amused despair. Delphine was determined to dramatize herself.

Chapter Two

A Very Different World

Delphine was still dramatizing herself by early evening, when her father and mother and Pelagia had gone off by car to the Thorburg Theatre and Edward and Anne were ready to go to the Opera House by Tube. She had lost the toss, to her mother's secret relief, for she had had a good many late nights and should be in bed early.

"I'm clearly the unlucky one of the family," she mourned, wandering into Anne's room, where her sister was putting the last touches to her appearance. Anne was wearing her favourite dress, a brilliant emerald green one, and was taking a little white shawl and a white evening bag.

"But you have looks and personality," Anne pointed out.

"They're all I have got, then. I've never won a toss in my life and it isn't fair."

Anne gave her a quick hug, which was received with frowning impatience.

"I'm awfully sorry, but you'll have lots more chances of going to Covent Garden. Think! A whole lifetime. You may even dance there yourself one day. So cheer up."

"She gets such awful moods," she said to Edward, as they walked rapidly down Baker Street in the hot, bright evening light. "Do you suppose it's the artistic temperament? You're quite placid and so am I."

"Pelagia isn't," said Edward, fishing out the money for the Underground tickets. "She gets moods. Think of the agony we went through when she took her exams and then was waiting to hear if she'd been accepted as a senior student. And then the first time she danced in *Coppélia*. The whole house was in a turmoil."

Anne frowned.

"I suppose we all get our uncertain times, though it is easier for you, being a boy. You're good, anyway, and they always want men in ballet. There's not really the faintest chance of your being thrown out on your ear. I got pretty worked up last year when they were choosing people for the Christmas Show, and sometimes it comes over me with a feeling of real terror that I may not turn into a good dancer. Mr Thorburg wouldn't allow the fact that Mother is a ballerina to influence him if we weren't good enough. But, going back to Delph, she sulks and moans and makes such a fuss. I only hope she settles down at the Thorburg and doesn't make a nuisance of herself."

"Oh, she'll be all right when she finds herself with a bunch of other new kids."

"She'll throw out her chest and remind them that Mother is Mona Garland, and that's a thing we've never done. We've shrunk from it, if anything. I've always thought it more of a disadvantage than an asset. People are so ready to say, 'One would think that Mona Garland's daughter could do better than that!' "

They travelled south-east on the Bakerloo Line, changed at Piccadilly and left the train at Covent Garden.

"I was glad that they thought we'd be too early if we went in the car," Anne remarked, as they left the lift, crossed the road and walked down Floral Street. "I love coming this way. There's such a feeling of urgency; everyone hurrying towards the Opera House." The street was very narrow and the pavement was crowded near the amphitheatre doors. "Really, you know, I love the Opera House far more than the Thorburg Theatre."

"That's heresy!" her brother said lightly, as they rounded the corner and moved into the crowded front entrance.

"Oh, I love the Thorburg, too. It almost seems to belong to us. But there's a sort of splendour here that the Thorburg never gets." And Anne gazed about her appreciatively as they went down a curving passage, up some side stairs and into the Stalls Circle. The big, semi-circular theatre burst on them, with its blazing lights, its great red and gold curtain and the tiers rising to the high domed roof.

They bought programmes and were shown to their seats in the front row, and Anne leaned on the ledge for a moment, staring round, her hair falling back from her clearcut face, with its green eyes and rather wide mouth. She and Edward made a handsome pair as they sat in solitude – for it was still quite early and a number of seats were empty – but neither of them noticed that a few people glanced up from the stalls and wondered who the red-haired boy and girl could be.

"Mona Garland's children," said a woman who wrote for one of the ballet magazines, to her companion.

"Really? They have a sort of air. They look like dancers."

"They're at the Thorburg School. I wrote an article about the whole family a few months ago – *The Ballet Family* – and met them all then. That's Anne, the middle girl. She's quite unselfconscious. Now if it were the youngest girl –"

"Is she at the Thorburg, too?"

"She's still pretty young, but she was hoping to go soon. She struck me as a minx. She'd never sit there and be unaware of attracting attention. She'd be smiling all round, as good as saying, 'Look at me!' "

Unaware of this conversation, Anne settled down to

study her programme, making careful note of who was dancing each role. It was true that she had seen *Giselle* many times, but it was one of her favourite ballets. In fact, she had seen most of the great classical and romantic ballets over and over again, as well as a large number of modern ones, but there was still always a thrill in the rising of the curtain, and she was well aware that no two performances were ever quite the same.

All the young Garlands had heard about and seen ballet from their earliest years. Anne's very first memory was of standing in the wings at the Thorburg Theatre watching her mother dance the Rose Adagio in *The Sleeping Beauty*. But, sitting in the Royal Opera House on that hot evening in September, she felt both excitement and a keen sense of anticipation. It mattered not a jot that she knew every movement in *Giselle*; they were going to see a very great dancer, a dancer far greater than their own mother, though Mona Garland had her own ardent following and was sure of her place in the ballet world.

"Won't it be wonderful for Joan to come to London and see ballet?" Anne said presently. "Perhaps she never has. How strange that must be. Once she gets over missing her mother she's sure to be thrilled. We can tell her so much."

"Perhaps she's like her mother and prefers the North. Maybe she *won't* be thrilled."

But that seemed to Anne an extraordinary and unlikely point of view and she would have argued it if the house-lights hadn't begun to fade. She would never have dreamed of speaking after that.

The orchestra was in its place in the vast, deep orchestra pit and applause broke out as the conductor appeared. Anne clasped her hands and sat back with a little sigh of contentment. The familiar music began to fill the great theatre and presently the curtain rose to show two little cottages and the backcloth of hills and a distant castle. And when Albrecht, disguised as the peasant Loys, knocked at the cottage door she held her breath until the ballerina appeared.

"Some day – some day it might be me," she thought, and after that her mind was entirely on the dancing before her, as the long ballet unfolded. She gave no more thoughts to the Lancashire cousin, who must be spending so different an evening more than two hundred miles away. All that mattered was Giselle, at first so happy and then gradually enveloped in tragedy. When the curtain came swishing down, at the end of the first act, with the villagers and the members of the Royal hunting-party grouped about the dead girl, Anne gave a long sigh and blinked as the lights came on.

"She *is* the greatest of them all. That mad scene – her flying black hair and the look on her face."

"Come up to the Crush Bar and have some coffee or an ice," said Edward, and, still blinking, Anne followed him up the stairs into the brilliant light of the chandeliers.

Two days later, on Monday evening, Joan Bradshaw escaped from the neighbour's house where she had been staying since Friday night, and made her way on to the hills above Watergrove Reservoir.

She climbed almost unthinkingly, scarcely noticing the familiar scene, for since her mother's death she had barely seemed conscious of anything but the dreadful ache in her chest. Besides, her eyes were so red and swollen from crying that the bright September light hurt them.

So she climbed up the old road, her sandalled feet stepping with sure instinct on the loose stones. Above her rose the high, bare hills ... Brown Wardle, Middle Hill, Hades, a long curving line under the soft blue sky.

Presently she took a little side path that had once been an important causeway over the hills into Yorkshire. It was

boggy and overgrown now, though here and there the smooth stones of the ancient, almost lost way showed for a few yards. Up and up and up, until at last she stopped on the crest of the ridge and flung herself down on the rough grass.

Now she did look about her, filled suddenly with the terrible knowledge that this was the last time. The last time she would ever be part of these bleak, lonely hills that she had known all her life and that she deeply loved.

It was all spread out in the bright light – the narrow little path up which she had come, the old road, the great shining stretch of the reservoir, green and gold rather than blue as the light deepened, and the town down in the valley.

This was the end. She felt rather as though she had died with her mother and that the Joan Bradshaw who went South with the unknown uncle would be some other girl.

Life had seemed so safe, so happy, in the little stone house on the hillside above the village of Wardle. There had not been much money, but they had managed very well, sharing many simple pleasures: walks on the moors, a Saturday trip down to Rochdale to shop and then go to the cinema, an occasional cheap holiday on the Yorkshire or

Lancashire coasts. She had liked her school and had been doing well there, and had always looked forward to her favourite lessons of English, history and art.

The thing that had happened so few days ago had found her utterly unprepared. Her father had died five years before, when she was eight, but it had been after a long illness. But for her mother to go so suddenly, leaving her quite alone …

Well, there were, of course, the London uncle, aunt and cousins, but they belonged to a different world, a world as far removed as if it were on another continent. Joan had only twice been to a big theatre, when she had been taken to the pantomime in Manchester, and it seemed fantastic, unbelievable, that she had an aunt who was a ballerina, an uncle who conducted an orchestra, and four cousins who were also going to be dancers.

She had always felt some curiosity about them, but had never been able to learn much, for her mother did not seem to wish to talk about them. She rarely even mentioned her own musical career, though a good piano was one of their few luxuries and she had given her daughter lessons for some years.

"It seems a daft sort of life to me," she had once said in

her downright way, referring to her brother and his family. She was not a Northerner, but she had absorbed the Lancashire temperament so thoroughly that few people had ever believed that she had been born and brought up in London.

"But awfully romantic," Joan had said, getting in reply the somewhat scornful retort: "I daresay it must seem so. People think the same about the life of a concert pianist, but quite soon I knew it wasn't for me. They said I had talent, but I never regretted giving it up. And I must say I never liked ballet. I loved opera, but, perhaps unreasonably, I never could swallow the ballet conventions. *Giselle* now; especially the second act. All those blessed Wilis drifting about in a blue light, and poor Albrecht dancing and dancing until he was exhausted. Not that he didn't deserve all he got."

"I wish I could see it, all the same," Joan had said slowly.

Since then she had seen ballet a few times on television. They had no set themselves, but she visited the house of a schoolfriend especially to see *Les Sylphides* and, on other occasions, *The Haunted Ballroom* and *The Rake's Progress*. She had been enchanted by the music and fascinated by the unfamiliar movements, but she still felt that the Garlands' world was utterly remote and impossible to understand. Still curious, she had read a life of Margot Fonteyn, but had been bewildered by the unfamiliar terms and so many references to ballets that she could hardly begin to imagine.

Then she had been taken with the rest of her class to Manchester to see an exhibition of designs for costumes and scenery, and, since she was very artistic, this had really fired her imagination. In the days that followed she had found herself mentally trying to create something of her own. It had never got further than that, but she had been left with a vivid image of a two-act ballet about the Jacobite Army marching south through Lancashire, the first act somewhere in the bleak hills and the second in Manchester. The music for it would have been arrangements of Jacobite airs and perhaps the song, *Farewell, Manchester*, though she had no real idea whether it would be possible to put ballet movements to them. She could see the two sets and some of the costumes in her mind's eye, but they had remained in her thoughts, for her school and home life left her little time for creative work.

Now she was to be pitchforked into the new world at a time when she felt utterly unable to face it.

"I want to stay here!" she said aloud, clasping her thin sun-tanned hands round her bare knees and tossing back her dark, slightly wavy hair. "I don't see why I can't stay with Mrs Thwaite. She wouldn't mind; I think she'd be glad to have me. The Garlands can't want me and I hate the very thought. I wish that Uncle Edwin had never come!"

But he *had* come, arriving in a hired car on Sunday morning and announcing that he was going to stay at a hotel down in Rochdale. He was a tall, good-looking man with thick greying hair and rather bushy eyebrows, and he was totally unlike the men she knew. He had been very kind, though Joan had been too shy and sunk in misery to respond at all. He had talked to Mrs Thwaite, found out the names of his sister's bank and lawyer, and promised to arrange the sale of the furniture. The house was rented; they had taken it when Joan's father died, as their own had been too large.

Joan had no watch, but she knew that it was getting late. Soon the sun would set and Mrs Thwaite would be expecting her to go back for her supper. She sighed and rose to her slim height – she was rather tall for thirteen – and took a great breath of the hill air. The last time …

But that way lay more sorrow, and she felt that she couldn't bear to cry any more. She set off downhill towards the old road and Watergrove, thinking with dread of the next day when the funeral would take place. Her uncle had said firmly that she was not to go. And then the journey to London. If she could have run away she would have done so, but she was a practical girl and it was obvious that, without money, she would not get very far.

No, it would have to be London and the Garlands. There was clearly nothing else for it, but if she had been going to the moon rather than to Moone Crescent she could hardly have felt it more distant and alien.

Chapter Three

Off to Coppélia

Mrs Thwaite and some of the other neighbours went to the funeral, but Joan was left alone, to finish packing her few possessions and to wait for her uncle to collect her in a hired car. The neighbours, she knew, thought it simply terrible that she wasn't to go to the funeral, and Joan herself agreed with them, but her uncle had said emphatically that, in his view, young people should never attend funerals.

"Some o' them rum London ideas," Mrs Thwaite had said. "Theatre folk – they're not like ordinary people, anyhow. I'm sure I hope you'll be happy with them."

Joan herself had no hope at all. By Tuesday morning she only knew that she had to face the ordeal of the strange household somehow.

So she finished packing her two very shabby suitcases and the big wooden box that was to follow by rail. In the box were the few household treasures that she had begged to keep: some vases, pictures and other small things, her own and her mother's books. Quite a number of the books had belonged to her father and she would not leave them to be sold with the furniture. She was saddest of all to think of losing the piano, but she had not even mentioned it. She felt, in any case, that she would never want to play again.

Then she put on her blue pleated skirt and paler blue blouse – another thing that upset Mrs Thwaite was that apparently the London uncle didn't believe in mourning, though there had, in fact, been no chance to buy any – and laid ready her blue school coat, beret and shabby gloves. It was a warm morning and there was really no need for a coat at all. Then she went outside and sat on the wall in front of Mrs Thwaite's little house next door, finding some comfort in the heat of the sun on her shoulders.

Presently she saw what must be the hired car approaching, and rose slowly. Mr Garland had given Mrs Thwaite and some of the other women a lift home, and she heard their voices below as she ran upstairs to put on her beret and seize the rest of her things.

"Your uncle's waiting, lass!" Mrs Thwaite called up.

When Joan descended the narrow stairs her cases were already in the car, and Mrs Thwaite enveloped her in a hug.

"Lunch in Manchester, he says, love, though I told him there was plenty of hot-pot. Take care of yourself and mind you come back to see us one day."

"I will. Oh, I will. And thank you for being so k-kind."

It was hard to face the rest of the goodbyes with composure, especially as two of the women were almost openly crying, but Joan found herself in the car and they drove away down the lane, through the rather grim little village and down towards Rochdale and the main Manchester Road. Mr Garland did not seem to want to talk and Joan was glad. She sat there staring out at the rows of stark little houses, at the familiar buildings and the encircling moors. It wasn't any of it beautiful – it was probably downright ugly, except for the moors themselves – but it was home and consequently very dear.

She had no idea with what deep depression her uncle

gazed on the same scene, marvelling that his sister had been happy in such a place. The people were kind, of course, but he had felt himself very much a fish out of water with them, and it would be a relief to get back to London with the child who sat so quietly beside him. He had visited the North many times when the Company was on tour, but that had been to Liverpool, Manchester or Newcastle, staying in big hotels and seeing almost nothing of his surroundings. The dark buildings, the canals, the smoke, the housing estates and the drab fields seemed to him like the end of the world, and as for that little dark-stoned village clinging below the hills ... a week in such a place would have seemed a kind of death, and yet his sister had voluntarily, even eagerly, made her home there.

Oh, well, thought Edwin Garland, as they drove slowly through the Manchester traffic, it no doubt took all sorts to make a world, but how would Joan Bradshaw react to their very different way of life? She had an intelligent face, and she was not bad-looking, but her clothes were dreadful, and he had not yet heard her say more than ten consecutive words.

They had a hurried lunch in a hotel that seemed to Joan very splendid, and then took their first-class seats on the express. They had the compartment to themselves and Edwin Garland settled himself comfortably in a corner with the newspapers he had bought.

He had also bought magazines for Joan, choosing ones that he thought his daughters liked, since she seemed to have no opinion in the matter. But when she showed no interest in reading them he remembered another paper that he had brought to show her. He opened his small case and handed her a copy of *Ballet Monthly* published the previous June.

"Look, dear. I thought you might like to see this. It may give you some idea of the children."

Joan took the magazine slowly. The cover picture was of a slim dancer wearing a short peasant skirt, a darker bodice and a brief white blouse, and the caption read: "Mona Garland as Swanilda in *Coppélia*".

Joan gasped, her hazel eyes opening very wide.

"But – but it *can't* be Aunt Mona!"

He laughed, pleased to see a spark of interest.

"Why not? Swanilda is one of her favourite roles. She's dancing it tonight."

"But – but she looks like a girl! She couldn't have four children and one who is – is seventeen."

He laughed again, amused by her awed and unbelieving tone.

"She has, all the same. I don't say that it's usual for a ballerina to have so many children. Some great dancers never marry at all, and others who do don't often have more than one child. But we happened to like large families and it didn't really affect her career so very much. She was always dancing again in a very few months. Of course we were lucky having Annali to look after us all, and there was a nanny as well when the children were very small. Now Annali just has a young Swiss cousin to help her. You'll like both Annali and Rosa. They come from Kandersteg in the Bernese Oberland. They'll tell you all about it. Poor Rosa's still rather homesick. She's only eighteen and she finds London strange after her village in the mountains."

Joan could well believe it. The thought of Rosa warmed her briefly as she turned the pages, which were packed with pictures of dancers of both sexes. After a few moments she found the article headed "The Ballet Family". There was another picture of Mona Garland, this time in a filmy white ballet dress. "Mona Garland dancing the Prelude from *Les Sylphide*", was printed underneath. Then there was a photograph of Edwin Garland conducting the Thorburg Orchestra, and one of Pelagia as an old-fashioned schoolgirl in *Graduation Ball*. "Pelagia Garland, who will not be eighteen until November, only recently joined the Thorburg Company," she read.

But it was at the three bottom pictures, spread over two pages, that Joan looked with the most interest. "Edward Garland, who is fourteen and a pupil at the Thorburg School, practises at the *barre* in the studio at the top of the house in Moone Crescent," said the caption. Then there was one of Anne, in tights and a leotard; and a head and shoulders portrait of Delphine.

Anne, with her straight hair tied back with a ribbon, looked so alive and confident that Joan's heart sank. Anne was thirteen – the cousin, surely, that she would get to know best – but she couldn't imagine being friendly with her. She looked nice, certainly, but so self-assured – she was important enough to have her picture in a real magazine. Delphine, smiling a little coyly into the camera, was undoubtedly the prettiest, with her curls and long-lashed eyes.

"Delphine's lovely," she said aloud, very shyly.

"Yes, she is pretty, isn't she? And I'm afraid she knows it. She's rather spoilt and we've been having a little trouble with her lately, but we hope she'll settle down when she starts at the Thorburg School on Thursday."

"She's only nine and she's already starting to be a dancer?"

"She's ten now and it's about the right age to start at a ballet school though some do join later, having just had a lesson or two a week. The girls will tell you all about it. We'll have to find a school for *you*, of course."

"I – I passed for a Grammar School. I expect I could be transferred. One of our girls moved to Birmingham and *she* was."

"Maybe. But I've been thinking that perhaps a private school would be best. There's a very good one not far away from us."

"But – but it would be too expensive."

"My dear, your mother had a little money of her own and it will come to you now, of course. You mustn't worry about money, anyway. We have enough. Your mother's money can be used for your education and for any training you may want later. Have you any ideas about what you'd like to be?"

"I've always thought that – that I'd like to teach."

He said kindly, opening the *Guardian*, "That sounds quite a good idea, but you have plenty of time to change your mind." And privately he wondered how on earth this pale, tense, serious child would fit into their necessarily somewhat unconventional household.

Joan was quick enough to read some, at least, of his thoughts, and as she read the article that accompanied the pictures she felt more and more dismayed. If she had been going to live in South America with a family that spoke Spanish the prospects couldn't have seemed much stranger.

She put down the magazine and sat staring blankly out of the windows, her heart heavy and her throat aching from suppressed emotion.

"Only last Friday everything was all right. Or I thought it was: Mother never told me that she was worse than I thought. Only last Friday we were talking about Christmas and saying we might go to that little hotel at Blackpool."

Life seemed very cruel and frightening, and she dreaded the arrival in London, though her uncle kept on looking at his watch and saying that he thought they were running late. It was cutting it rather fine, in any case, as they had to get from Euston to Moone Crescent and then he had to change for the evening performance.

"The ballet doesn't start until seven-thirty, but we have to be there by seven, at the very latest. We'll have tea on the train and I'm afraid it will mean going straight off to the theatre. You'll get used to our dashing off to classes and rehearsals and actual performances, but I'm sorry it had to happen on your first evening. Edward and the others will look after you and maybe you'll be glad to go to bed early."

Joan didn't answer. She couldn't have done, even if there had been anything to say.

Meanwhile, at Moone Crescent, life had gone on much as usual. On Monday morning, after her usual class (there was no Company rehearsal), Mona Garland had borne Delphine off to the large West End store that stocked the Thorburg School uniform. As luck would have it the green school suit and paler green blouses had fitted Delphine without alteration. The cloak that every member of the School wore at times about the building was rather long, but Annali would alter it in time for Thursday; and leotards, tights and other necessities all, fortunately, fitted. Several new pairs of ballet shoes were added to the many parcels, but Delphine's difficult mood did not lift. She was at her most annoying and aggressive, showing off in front of the assistants and deliberately displaying a marked lack of interest in everything that was bought.

Mona Garland bore it as long as she could and then said in a low voice, "Look, Delph! If you were smaller you'd get a rare smack for this, and well you know it. I know that your pride took a tumble – in many ways the whole thing was unfortunate – but there's no need to take it out on me. You *want* to go to the Thorburg, so let's have an end to this play-acting. You might remember that I've just spent a lot of money on your new things, and we also have to pay a term's fees at your old school."

"I don't see why I should be grateful, Mother. I don't want to go. I've told you."

"Well, anyway, behave yourself in public, and behave yourself when you get to the Thorburg, too, or you'll shame us all. They'll expect more of you because you're the last of the Garlands. That's hard, but true, and you may as well face up to it."

"I don't see why I had to be born last."

"Nothing can alter it, anyway. If you want some advice, though I doubt it, being you, you'll stay quiet and retiring for a few weeks."

"Anne and Edward keep on saying that. Why should I? I'm me and I'm not retiring by nature."

And Mona Garland laughed and sighed and wondered why it was that Delphine had turned out so different from the others. But she could not give very much more thought to Delphine just then, because there was much else to occupy her mind. For one thing she had remembered on Sunday, with quite a sickening jolt, that she, her husband and Pelagia were going on tour in a fortnight's time. The Company was going to France, Switzerland and Italy and they would all be away for several weeks. Nothing could have been more unfortunate with a new addition to the household, and she only hoped, as she and Delphine carried the parcels to the car, that Joan Bradshaw would settle down quickly. Poor child, she would probably need mothering, and that was just what she was unlikely to get, with the best will in the world.

Anne spent the whole of Monday with her great friend Lisa Thorburg, Johann Thorburg's daughter. The Thorburg family had originally been Swiss, and it was through them that Annali had come to the newly married Garlands so long ago. Johann Thorburg still retained a trace of his original accent and could never have been taken for an Englishman, but Lisa was wholly English in outlook and appearance – a brown-haired, blue-eyed, often serious girl, who had been at the School since she was ten and was a fairly good dancer.

Anne loved Lisa and had thought until recently that she

understood her pretty well, but for the past few months Lisa had had moods that distressed and disturbed her. Asked what was the matter she had shrugged and said that it was no good talking about it, and the result was that Anne felt farther from her friend than she had ever done since that day when they had both been new together in the lowest class at the Thorburg. They had become friendly at once, perhaps because both shared a slight problem – the fact that one was the daughter of the Director of the School and Company and the other the daughter of a famous ballerina.

It had meant behaving carefully, as they had both known, when only just ten, and that was why Anne had tried to advise Delphine.

The holidays were drawing to a close and on Thursday they would be back at school, so Anne and Lisa were determined to enjoy themselves. They went by boat up the Thames to Kew Gardens, where they ate a picnic lunch then returned in the late afternoon, had tea in the West End and went to a film.

It was a lovely sunny day and on the surface they were happy and light-hearted, but Anne had the feeling that Lisa was not wholly with her. But when she said tentatively, during tea, "There *is* something! I wish you'd tell me!" Lisa answered lightly: "I will one day. One day I shall have to, when I've plucked up the courage."

"But, Lisa, it's silly! I thought we told each other everything?"

"I haven't got it clear yet. Perhaps I never shall."

"Wouldn't it help to talk about it?"

"No, it wouldn't. Not yet. If we don't hurry we'll be late for the film."

They had paid their bill and hurried off to the cinema in Leicester Square.

By Tuesday the little room next to the studio was ready for

Joan, and Anne was feeling both excited and uneasy about the arrival of their unknown cousin. After lunch Delphine went off to a friend's house and Edward announced that he was having tea with Jocheli Thorburg and Gilbert Whitton at the Thorburgs' house near Primrose Hill and might be back late. Jocheli Thorburg went to a Grammar School and was, to his father's great distress, totally uninterested in ballet, but Gilbert was at the School.

"I thought you'd be here to help to entertain your cousin," Mona Garland said, with a small frown creasing her usually smooth brow.

"Anne can do that. She's nearest Joan in age."

"Yes, but it looks awful if we're all out this evening. Even if the train's on time there isn't going to be too much time. I think I shall pack your father's clothes and he can change at the theatre. Joan just won't understand the urgency of our lives."

'She'll learn," said Edward darkly.

"Poor child, no doubt she will. But –"

"Anne'll manage, and the fewer of us the better, perhaps. All of us might be overpowering."

"Perhaps," agreed his mother. "But it seems a poor welcome."

Anne spent the afternoon in a state of restlessness. She spoke to a few of her friends on the telephone, switched on the television for five minutes and then switched it off again, took Bonne-Bouche for a walk round Queen Mary's Garden, and then sat in the garden and read, without concentrating very well on the story.

Six o'clock came and passed. On the evenings when there was a performance they had a high tea at half-past five and then there was the usual bustle of getting ready for the theatre. By half-past six Mona Garland was anxious and more restless than her daughter, and Pelagia had gone off by Tube.

"If your father doesn't come soon I shall have to go."

"Oh, *Mother*!" Anne groaned. "What shall I do with her?"

"She'll want to unpack and Annali will give her a meal. She can go to bed early. I expect she'll be glad to."

"But it's such a responsibility."

"I'm sure you can cope with it." Mona Garland sounded as though her thoughts were far away and Anne was well aware of her pre-performance mood. It was just no good arguing. When they were small children they had always been kept out of the way, except for a goodnight kiss.

At twenty-five to seven a taxi drew up at the door and there was her father with a tall, thin girl in a navy-blue coat and beret.

"Thank goodness!" cried Mona Garland. She had already fetched the car and now they could be off. She was waiting in the hall, slim and cool-looking in spite of her anxiety to be off to the theatre, when Edwin Garland entered with Joan.

To Joan, enveloped for a moment in a sweet-smelling hug, she looked like a being from another world. Sleek red hair under a tiny hat made of green flowers, wide green eyes, a dress obviously straight from Paris. The hug had been kindly, even warm, but it only made the homesick girl remember her own mother with a terrible pang. Her mother who had gone off to hospital in her old grey dress, with her soft dark hair all awry.

"Here you are, Joan! And we're very, very glad to have you. Your uncle will have explained about the need to get to the theatre. Anne will look after you. Here she is. And Annali. You must be tired and hungry. Oh, and here's Bonne-Bouche to welcome you, too."

Joan looked round in hopeless bewilderment. The elegant little crescent, the equally elegant white and scarlet-painted hall of the strange house, the capering

poodle with the extraordinary name, the strange people ... It was too much. It was awful! And her uncle had whirled upstairs, rushed down again with a suitcase and was hurrying out to the car in a way that showed he had already forgotten all about her. At least he was someone a little familiar in this new world, and now he had gone. The car started up and was driven rapidly away round the crescent.

"You must think we're rather mad," said Anne, shy and suddenly unusually awkward in the presence of this pale, unhappy-looking cousin.

"And sometimes she wouldn't be far out," said the grey-haired elderly woman, stepping from the background. "Down, Bonne! Look, I'll take your cases upstairs and then you must have something to eat."

"No, thank you. I – I had tea on the train."

"Well, we all know what train teas are like. A toasted bun and dry bread and butter. You'd better have some soup and scrambled eggs." She was already mounting the stairs, with Anne and Joan following. Up one flight, then another, and finally up a few narrower stairs.

"At the top, I'm afraid, but very quiet. There is only the studio up here. There! Now I'll go and heat the soup. Bring her down, Anne, in five minutes."

The little guest-room faced the back, with a view of narrow gardens and much higher buildings. The evening sunlight was streaming in, showing up the clear yellow and pale green of the decorations.

"It's pretty," said Joan with difficulty. It was about as different as it could possibly have been from her own small room at home, with its shabby, nondescript curtains and bedcover, home-made rug and window that looked far away to the buildings of Rochdale and Littleborough.

"Mother says you can put up your own pictures, if you have any, or else buy some that you like," Anne offered, perching on the edge of the bed.

"Oh, thank you. Yes, I – I have some. They're coming on by rail. In a big box – I left it at Mrs Thwaite's." Joan took off her coat, in which she was far too hot, put it, her beret and shabby little bag on a chair, and looked round helplessly.

"I shouldn't bother to do anything now. Would you like to wash on the way down? There are two bathrooms, but both below. Unfortunately this is the only room that hasn't got a fitted basin. Mother has kept on saying that we ought to have one put in."

"Yes, please." Joan felt dreadfully dirty from the train. The fact that she knew that she looked grubby, untidy and dowdy added a little to her despair. Anne, with her shining hair, crisp yellow and white spotted dress and neat sandals, looked smart, alert and sure of herself.

But Anne was not really sure of herself at all. She felt deeply indignant with Edward and Delphine for leaving her to cope with the new cousin alone.

"Come on, then. Annali hates food to be kept waiting. You can unpack afterwards."

Joan felt that food would choke her, but couldn't make any more protests. So she managed to swallow the soup and scrambled eggs, while Anne sat on the sofa near by, chattering uneasily to break the awkward silences.

"It's *Coppélia* tonight. I suppose Father told you? Mother doesn't always dance, of course. Usually not more than three or four times a week and often less. But she always has a class in the mornings, and there are often rehearsals."

"Do you mean that – she teaches dancing as well?"

Anne stared.

"Teaches? No, of course not. She attends a class. Everyone does."

"But I thought she was a great ballerina?"

"They all go to classes, all the same, just as long as they keep on dancing. There are going to be a lot of rehearsals from now on, because in just over a fortnight's time the Company is going abroad. They're going to Paris and Basle and Zurich and Milan and Monte Carlo."

"Your mother and father and Pelagia?"

"All of them, lucky things."

"And you – we – stay here?"

"Oh, of course. It often happens. In the spring they went to Australia and New Zealand. Mother and Father, that is; Pel wasn't in the Company then. Annali looks after us." Anne held out her arms to the black poodle, who bounded into them, quivering all over with pleasure. "Do you like Bonne-Bouche? She's our darling."

"She's very nice, but what an odd name."

"Well, we said she had to have a ballet one. It's a Cranko ballet."

"Cranko?"

"John Cranko. The choreographer. You must have heard of him?"

"No." And then Joan pushed her plate away and said in a kind of burst, "I haven't heard of anything. I don't know the first thing about ballet."

They stared at each other. Though Anne had thought herself prepared for the new cousin's ignorance on the subject, now that it came to the point it seemed to her unbelievable.

"You'll soon learn," she said awkwardly, after a few moments. "I'm afraid we think of nothing else. It's inevitable. But you must have been able to see some ballet where you lived. In Manchester, anyway. The Royal Ballet goes there, and most other companies. I believe it's a couple of years since the Thorburg danced there."

"I – I don't know. I hardly ever went to Manchester. I've only been to the theatre two or three times in my life. To see the pantomime at Christmas."

"In your whole *life*?"

"Yes. We – we had other things to do, more important." Joan's tone was suddenly belligerent in the face of Anne's blank surprise.

The words "But what could be more important?" quivered on Anne's lips, but she didn't say them. She certainly must not quarrel with this tense and clearly miserable girl. She felt very sorry for her, but was dismayed as well.

She put Bonne-Bouche down and rose, smoothing her crisp skirts.

"If you've had enough to eat perhaps we'd better unpack your things. Mother said you might like to go to bed early."

Chapter Four

Meeting Nowhere

Anne had had every intention of helping Joan to unpack, but she quickly sensed that she was not wanted, and drifted away. When Delphine came home she was sitting on the stairs facing the front door, too restless and disturbed to settle to anything.

Delphine had enjoyed her day and looked more cheerful. "What are you sitting there for?"

"I don't know. Waiting for you or Edward. I think you were both jolly mean to desert."

"Has she come?"

"Of course she has. She's unpacking. You'd better go up and introduce yourself. And be *nice* to her. She needs it badly."

"I'm always nice," said her sister complacently.

"Well, this is one time when it's necessary. She's shy and miserable and a bit cross and she doesn't know *anything* about ballet, she says. I honestly thought I was prepared for that, but now – Well!"

"Oh, but she must! She's thirteen."

"My child, that's nothing to go by. She says she's had more important things to think about. Oh, I felt so helpless. That's one thing *you* won't be."

Delphine bounded up the stairs and was away some time. When she came down again she looked unusually subdued.

"I was nice, but she wouldn't talk. She's got her things all spread about. What funny clothes she has!"

"What do you mean?"

"All navy blue or grey and no pretty undies."

"I expect Mother will get her some. Perhaps it was too cold in the North, and things get dirty there."

"Dirtier than London?"

"I don't know, really. I've always thought it was dirty. Oh, here's Edward!"

Edward came in, whistling.

"Why the meeting on the stairs? Can I join?"

"You should have joined long ago," said Anne, rather bitterly. "You might have known what to say. She's come and I've made a mess of things somehow. She's not a bit like a usual sort of girl."

"Perhaps it's you who is unusual."

Anne frowned.

"I've always thought myself quite ordinary."

"We live in a narrow world. Does that occur to you?"

"No. No, it hadn't. It seems quite a wide world. I thought it was hers that was narrow."

"Well, it probably was, but she may be nearer to reality."

"I suppose it depends on what *is* reality."

"So it does. Better go and fetch her down. Is she unpacking?"

But Annali appeared then and swept them aside.

"That poor young thing! She must go to bed and have a long night. I will see to her."

They gave in thankfully, watching the straight back of their household martinet disappearing round the curve of the stairs. It was a relief, to Anne at least, to have responsibility removed.

Everyone but Annali was in bed and asleep by the time

that Mr and Mrs Garland and Pelagia returned from the theatre, and Annali reported that Joan had gone to bed early and that she had tucked her in herself.

"She's unhappy and not very well. I should not disturb her."

"I suppose she'll settle down," said Edwin Garland, with a tired sigh. It had been a long and troublesome day, though the performance had gone off reasonably well.

"She's probably still suffering from shock," said his wife, as Annali began to hand round the cold supper that was always waiting. "We'll have to be very nice to her, and it ought to help that she'll be seeing London for the first time. I only wish, though, that we weren't going away so soon."

"Perhaps in a way it may be for the best. It will give the younger ones a real chance to get to know her. I shouldn't worry too much. I should think she's basically a very practical young thing."

"A bit of practicality in this household might be a good thing,' said Pelagia, biting hungrily into a chicken sandwich.

"Aren't *we* practical, then?"

"Perhaps. But a bit of northern commonsense ... Look at Delph."

But no one particularly wanted to think of Delphine then and they soon went upstairs.

Joan, who had been asleep, woke up and heard voices on the landing below. She crept out of bed and opened the door quietly, hearing a young, clear voice saying: "Actually I thought that the Mazurka was taken too slowly. It didn't seem to have its usual lilt and drive. And I thought that Prayer looked as though she'd been hypnotized. She had such a glassy stare."

"She's very promising. I thought she did well. Wait till you get your chance, Pel. You may look a bit 'glassy' the first time. What's the rehearsal tomorrow?"

"Oh, you know. *Peter* and a run through of *Graduation Ball*. For Saturday matinée, of course."

"Did you hear that Johann's decided to add the second act of *Lac* to the repertoire for the tour, after all?"

"I suppose that's because he always says that Odette's one of your best roles."

"He's not alone in that, but I do think that the second act has been overdone. Every company has it in its repertoire. Oh, well, sleep well!" And the silent stranger up above heard mother and daughter going to their different rooms.

Joan crept back to bed, once more feeling that if the Garlands had spoken an unknown language it could not have been much more difficult. What had all that been about? Somebody called Prayer – how odd! Who looked glassy-eyed. Somebody else called Peter, or was that a ballet? And what on earth was Lack? *Lac*, perhaps, she supposed, staring unhappily into the darkness. There seemed to be a lot of French used in ballet. Yes, there had been quite a bit in the Fonteyn book about a ballet called *Swan Lake* or *Le Lac des Cygnes*.

In search of desperately-needed comfort she began to think about the hills near her home, and, wandering in imagination on the high rough grass of Hades Hill, she did eventually go to sleep again.

Mona Garland arrived in Joan's room about ten past eight, wearing a beautiful, gold-coloured housecoat.

"Good morning, dear. Did you sleep well? I was so sorry to rush away last night, but you know how it is. Breakfast at half-past eight, as Pelagia has to be off to her class and rehearsal, and I have a class, too. And tomorrow, of course, the others will be starting school again. It's lucky there's one day between. I'm afraid you'll be lonely until we can arrange about a school for you."

"Oh, no. I – I shan't mind." In fact loneliness seemed to Joan highly preferable to facing the whole family at breakfast.

"Anyway, today you must get at least a glimpse of London. I expect Anne will take you around."

The morning sun was streaming into the dining-room when Joan appeared, wearing a blue and white cotton dress and very shabby sandals. A place had been laid for her between Anne and Edward, and Edward was introduced, then Pelagia.

"The only ones you haven't met. Oh, and Rosa," as a brown-haired, rosy-faced girl came in with fresh toast. "You come from the hills and Rosa from the mountains, so perhaps you can compare notes."

Joan and Rosa smiled shyly at each other and Joan felt that here, perhaps, was a friend, someone who would understand the dreadful homesickness that filled her.

The others – well, the whole family looked like people out of a magazine; they *were* in a magazine! Even the sunny, very modern room looked like something out of a magazine, to Joan's eyes. And yet everyone looked friendly, especially Edward, who was very good-looking and had a nice smile.

They plied her with food that she didn't want – their appetites amazed her; she had yet to learn that dancers eat prodigiously – and then seemed to forget her, to her acute relief. The talk was all about the theatre and people she didn't know, even by name.

The poodle sat engagingly on a chair near by, head cocked hopefully, and once Delphine passed her a piece of bacon.

"Oh, don't feed her at the table, Delph! She has enough naughty habits."

"She's hungry." Delphine tossed her curls. Clearly she disliked being corrected.

"She certainly isn't. Don't be silly! Now what is everyone doing today?"

Edward, it seemed, was going swimming and would not be back for lunch. Delphine was going back to her friend's house after lunch. Edwin Garland had an appointment and would probably not be home until the middle of the afternoon.

Anne sat in silence, feeling dismayed. What an idiot she had been not to invite Lisa over, or else to arrange to go out somewhere. She shot an indignant look from Delphine to Edward, but neither was looking in her direction.

"Then Anne's the free one," said Mona Garland. "Perhaps you and Joan and Delph could all help Annali by doing the shopping this morning? And then, Anne, you could take Joan around a little this afternoon. Remember she hasn't seen anything of London yet. You could go down to Piccadilly Circus and then walk through to Trafalgar Square, and perhaps round by the river a little and up Kingsway. I expect she'd like to see the Thorburg Theatre, and then you could go on to Russell Square and give her a glimpse of the School."

Anne was still sorry for Joan, but her heart sank. It was all very well her mother suggesting conducted tours, but it was the last precious day of the holidays.

"Shall I telephone Lisa and ask her to come, too?"

"Didn't Lisa tell you? She and her mother are going to see their aunt at Princes Risborough today. Johann mentioned it last night."

"No, she didn't," said Anne, defeated.

She got her mother alone while Joan was upstairs, making her bed.

"Mother, I don't mean to be horrid, but I don't know what to *say* to her. She looks so sad and last night I tried to talk, but it wasn't a bit of good."

Mona Garland was getting ready to hurry off to her class. She waved a bright lipstick impatiently.

"Oh, Anne *dear*, you can usually talk. Show her things,

tell her about London, find out what interests her."

"I do want to, but I don't know where to start."

"I'm afraid you'll have to, though. This afternoon I've got to see about some new costumes for the tour. That poor child! Try and make her laugh. She thinks we're ogres, or at any rate very peculiar."

On her knees by her newly-made bed, Joan was scribbling a letter to Mrs Thwaite.

"This is a lovely house, tall and narrow and painted white outside, with a bright red door. The houses are nearly all pretty and you can just see the park from some of the front windows. It's Regent's Park, where the Zoo is, and it looks enormous. So far that's all I've seen of London, except for Euston Station last night and the Euston Road, which was very busy and rather ugly, except just by Euston Square, where there are trees.

I just don't know what to tell you about the Garlands. Aunt Mona is beautiful and wears lovely clothes. She's not in the least like anyone I've met before. She has a nice voice and seems very kind, but she's always busy. Edward looks very nice, but I haven't said more than 'How do you do?' to him. I thought that boys who dance must be sort of peculiar, but he looks quite normal. Big and sun-tanned, with well-shaped hands.

Anne is going to take me to see London this afternoon. I'm afraid she doesn't want to, and that makes me feel bad. If I didn't feel so strange and so homesick I suppose I should be thrilled to see Piccadilly Circus and all the rest.

They have a dog with a very silly name. A ballet one.

I don't know what you'd think about it all. They think of nothing but ballet and I don't know what they're talking about half the time. It's a bit like being in a play when you haven't been told anything about your part.

Oh, I shall often think of home and the hills. London

seems so crowded, in spite of the park.

Thank you very, very much for being so kind to me and give my love to everyone.

JOAN."

She was writing the address on the envelope when Anne came in.

"Look! We're going shopping in a little while, but you haven't seen the house properly yet. Come and see our rooms. Oh, and this is the studio next door to you."

Joan gaped at the big light room, bare but for the *barre* along the wall, a huge mirror, a piano in a corner and a record-player and a case of records.

"Is this – where you dance?"

"We all practise here sometimes. We do exercises at the *barre* – like this." And Anne ran over to demonstrate a few *pliés*, then showed the five positions.

"But your mother does much harder things than that?"

"All dancers do the same. If they're young or quite old." Anne was determined to make her cousin understand. "Every day, every month, every year – always – the same exercises over and over again. It's to make your body pliant. It takes nearly ten years to make a dancer; that's why they start so young, and then they have to keep on afterwards. Even Pavlova, Markova, Fonteyn, Mother."

"But don't they get bored? That's drudgery." Joan was appalled to learn that it was such unending work as this that made those leaping, airy figures she had seen on the television screen.

"No, of course not," said Anne, and then added honestly, "anyone who cares knows that they just must practise endlessly. It's the only way, something that you just know from the first. But some can't stand it. We've had girls (and boys, too) leave the school because they can't. They get bored, and then they think, like you, that it's drudgery. They want time to do other things. But it doesn't often happen."

"Mrs Thwaite would say it was proper daft," said Joan. "Even Mother – Mother would have done."

"Come and see my room," said Anne hastily, seeing sorrow gathering at the mention of her mother. "I sleep here with Pelagia. That's her bed and these are her books and things and these are mine. This is my mascot. Pel's is that little ivory elephant." And she took up a tiny doll, dressed in a pink tutu and pink ballet shoes.

"Your mascot?"

"Yes, we all have them. Mother's is a ballet shoe that Pavlova wore. She got it when she was very young. Wasn't she lucky? If *I* could have Pavlova's shoe ... But I like my doll. She'll go everywhere with me when I get into the Company. *If* I do, of course. And when I was in the Christmas Show last year she sat by my make-up box."

"But that's superstition!" The rather shocked words were out before Joan could stop them and she saw Anne's eyes fly wide open. The remark had sounded impossibly smug.

"Of course it is. Don't sound as though we're practising black magic. Theatre folk are very superstitious. You know all the feeling there is about *Macbeth*, and never saying the last line of a play until the actual first night, and – do you think that daft, too?"

"I shan't ever understand," said Joan and they eyed each other, both conscious of the enormous invisible barrier. Delphine and Bonne-Bouche saved them by arriving with a rush.

"Come *on*, if you're coming! I've got the shopping list and three baskets. Annali says will you kindly hurry up as she wants the meat for lunch."

Both the older girls turned with relief and Joan ran to get her bag and the letter for Mrs Thwaite. When she was out of earshot Anne turned indignantly to Delphine.

"You might have helped me to look after her today! Why should it be me? It's a family thing, after all –"

"Ask Edward," said Delphine, twirling annoyingly.

"I can't. He's shot off. Really, families can be mean!"

"You're the same age, that's why."

"It's about the only thing we have in common, then," said poor Anne, and, a few minutes later, the shopping expedition set off.

Anne, at least, found it rather embarrassing to have a nearly silent companion. Misery and bewilderment were making Joan look more sulky than anything else, and Anne could not guess that she was finding it quite enough to absorb the London atmosphere and the alien accents without making an effort to cope with her companions.

She was equally silent over lunch and Mona Garland glanced at her anxiously. But she hoped that the girl would gradually relax and she gave Anne plenty of money as she saw them off.

"Have some tea out and better get taxis if you feel like it, just for once, Bunchy. Though Joan may prefer the buses and Tubes. After all, she'll have to learn how to get about."

It was another glorious afternoon and both girls set off without coats. Watching them walk away around the crescent Mona Garland made a mental note that, whatever else she did before the tour, she must see that her niece had some new clothes. She enjoyed dressing girls and had been sorry when Pelagia, achieving independence, had not asked her advice any more. Pelagia, in fact, spent most of her time in jeans and sweaters, since a good part of her life was spent in the dusty backstage regions of the Thorburg Theatre or else in the Company rehearsal rooms, a short distance away.

Anne and Delphine both liked pretty clothes. It would be fun, if only she could make time for it, to find just the right clothes for Joan, who would benefit from some good clothes. But it would have to be done tactfully, for she sensed that a strong pride lay behind Joan's quiet and withdrawn exterior.

Anne and Joan caught a bus in Baker Street that would take them to Piccadilly Circus. Anne conscientiously pointed out Portman Square, and some of the big shops in Oxford Street and Regent Street, but was not sure how much her companion was taking in. In fact, Joan was more than a little appalled by the thought of the vastness of London, by the hurrying crowds and the dust, noise and heat.

But she was thrilled – though she did not say so – to stand in Piccadilly Circus. It gave her a strange feeling of being in the centre of the world, but she doubted if she would ever come to terms with the city that Anne seemed to take so much for granted.

Joan dithered in the traffic as they crossed Regent Street and then Piccadilly, and Anne hauled her along by the arm, saying reassuringly: "It's all right. I won't let you get run over. You should see it in the rush hour; this is nothing. We'll go down Lower Regent Street and into the Mall. It's quieter there."

They stood on the Waterloo Steps above the Mall and for the first time a brief feeling of happiness filled Joan. For it really was beautiful and impressive – the great cream buildings on either side, the wide road below, the trees in St James's Park, as yet scarcely beginning to show autumn colours, and the misty blue towers of Westminster.

London! This was London! Her mother had always promised that they would come one day for a brief visit, but neither had ever imagined that Joan would come alone, for good. The thought took away the feeling of sudden happiness and Anne, seeing her face, said hastily: "We'll walk up to Admiralty Arch and then you'll see Trafalgar Square. You'll like the fountains and the pigeons and all

the people. The National Gallery, too, and St Martin's."

For the whole of that golden September afternoon Anne conscientiously pointed out things of interest. They walked down Whitehall, then stood on Westminster Bridge for a time before walking on towards Waterloo Bridge along the Embankment. They sat on a seat in the Victoria Embankment Gardens, for Joan, tireless on the Lancashire moors, found the hot pavements very hard on her feet. Then they went up to the Strand, into Aldwych and along the wide stretch of Kingsway to where the Thorburg Theatre stood, just past the Tube station. At the front of the theatre many notices and large posters were displayed, and Joan stared in awe and renewed astonishment at a poster that showed Mona Garland as Aurora in *The Sleeping Beauty*. It seemed extraordinary that this youthful-looking and famous woman was her aunt, the very person who had seen them off from the house in Moone Crescent.

"It must be so – so odd to have her for a mother," she said slowly.

"Well, I suppose we're used to it, you know. We grew up with the thought, of course. But I expect you'll find, when you go to school, that people will be awfully interested to find she's your aunt. Come round to the stage-door and see if we can get in."

"Into the theatre?"

"Of course. Why not?" And Anne led the way round into the narrow alleyway where the stage-door was. She thrust her head into the little office and said cheerfully: "Hello, Ned! This is my cousin, Joan Bradshaw. She's come to live with us, so you may see her often. All right if we go in?"

A little elderly man in his shirt sleeves looked out at her.

"Everyone's just gone, Miss Anne. The rehearsal went on for a tidy time. Yes, go along in, but don't be long. I'm going off home for a couple of hours."

The passage was long and dark after the sunlight, and filled with the smell of new wood, dust, grease-paint and a good many other aromas, not all of them pleasant. But Anne sniffed and laughed.

"Isn't it the loveliest smell in the world? If I was brought in blindfolded I'd know I was in a theatre. Look! I'll show you Mother's dressing-room. It's the best one, of course, nearest the stage."

Joan gazed in silence round the dressing-room, which was shabby and in no way splendid. She had vaguely imagined the ethereal beings of the ballet housed amid velvet and flowers and she was astonished to find everywhere so depressing.

She followed Anne into the wings and then on to the stage, which was cold and depressingly illuminated by a single harsh working light.

"This is the set for the Prologue of *The Sleeping Beauty*. They're dancing it tonight, but with Barbary Brown as Aurora – not Mother. Barbary's a good dancer, full of personality, but really better in character parts. Her dancing isn't quite lyrical enough for her to be absolutely tip-top in the great classical roles." And then, gazing round, she proceeded to add a spate of even more incomprehensible details about battens, flies, limes, floats and the iron.

"I thought it would be all so romantic," Joan said helplessly.

"Well, but it is, really," said the ballerina's daughter, who had breathed the air of the Thorburg Theatre since she was a few weeks old. "Not a fairy kind of romance, of course, in spite of what some outsiders think, but a real, down to earth kind. That's true, in spite of sore feet and the smell of sweat, and having to dance when you'd sooner go to bed with a hot water bottle. It's a tough, hard life and I have no illusions about it, but I still want it more than anything in the world."

Soon after that they left the theatre and continued north towards Russell Square. By then Anne was tired and thoroughly dispirited. She had tried her hardest, but it didn't seem to have done much good, and it was all too painfully clear that she and Joan would never have anything in common.

The Thorburg School was in Russell Square, a big building painted blue. Outside there was a large board with the words:

THORBURG BALLET SCHOOL
FULLY EDUCATIONAL.
INFORMATION FROM JOHANN THORBURG
OR THE HEADMISTRESS

To Anne it was the most important place in the world, and quite her most triumphant moment so far had been that day, more than three years before, when she had climbed the steps as a pupil for the first time.

But to Joan, fresh from a huge northern Grammar School that was the pride of the district, it did not look impressive. Some obscure emotion – perhaps envy of Anne's calm, happy acceptance of her world – made her say: "I thought it would be much bigger. It's – why, it's only two houses and the paint's peeling."

Anne bristled. She knew that the Thorburg was shabby and that there was not a great deal of money behind it, but to have a stranger criticize ... It was too much!

"What do you mean? It's the best ballet school in the world! Well, one of the best."

"At my school at home we had huge playing-fields, and a separate gym and lab and a wonderful art room ..."

"We don't need playing-fields. We don't play games. And there's a lot more behind. All sorts of built-on bits." Anne saw, out of the tail of her eye, a cruising taxi and spun round to signal to it. "Regent Palace Hotel please," she said crisply to the driver and hauled Joan in.

Her mother had said have tea, so they had better have it, but she only wished the day to be over. Tomorrow, entering the Thorburg once again, life would return to its usual happy normality.

They were very silent over the meal and when they came out the rush hour was still in full swing. Anne crossly contemplated letting Joan experience the Tube, but that would only be an obscure attempt to punish both of them. They had been given money, after all, and it wasn't often that she was able to ride in taxis. So they went along to the rank and climbed into the first taxi available.

It was a slow journey and Joan sat hunched in a corner, conscious of the hard lump in her throat. When, at last, they reached Moone Crescent and were let in by Rosa she just managed to mumble: "Thank you very much for taking me, Anne!" and then she ran upstairs, locked her bedroom door behind her, and flung herself down on the bed.

She knew, as well as Anne, that so far they met nowhere.

Chapter Five

New Term at Ballet School

That evening towards bedtime Mona Garland said to Joan: "Tomorrow afternoon, dear, we're going to see the headmistress of your new school. It's called the Scott-Smithson School and isn't very far away."

"I – I wish I could go to a Grammar School," Joan got out. She dreaded the thought of some snobbish London private school.

"But you'll like the Scott-Smithson. It's got a splendid reputation. If any of the girls hadn't wanted to dance I always thought they could go there. It's the sort of school that gives older girls every chance to specialize, as well as giving a good general education. In the morning, after my class, I thought we might do a little shopping. We have to see about your uniform, for one thing, and, with luck, some of the things may fit you without alteration. The term starts next Tuesday, so there isn't too much time. I also thought you might like one or two new dresses and a winter coat for best and so on."

Joan blushed vividly, and Mona Garland was glad that they were alone.

"There's no need, really. If I'm to have school things –"

"But wouldn't you like some pretty dresses and blouses

and underclothes? I do so love buying things for girls. Of course you'll have your own ideas, but if you'll let me help –"

"It's very – very kind of you." Joan gave in because she was all too well aware that her clothes were hopeless. She had grown so fast during the summer that most of her things were too short and skimpy and she had no winter coat at all, except for her shabby navy-blue school one. It felt like charity, but her uncle had seemed sure that she would have some money, and probably she wasn't justified in shaming the Garlands by her appearance. Pride urged her to insist that she could manage as she was, but her more sensible side caused her to agree before pride could get the upper hand. Besides, she had often longed secretly for pretty clothes, and if a famous ballerina wanted to dress her … Oh, well, what did it matter? Nothing mattered much.

Mona Garland sought Anne out just after she had retired to bed and found her in her dressing-gown, brushing her hair and frowning into the looking-glass.

"How did it go this afternoon, Bunchy?"

"Badly, I'm sorry."

"I was afraid so."

"Mother, I did honestly try, but she doesn't know *anything*. I think she liked bits of London, but she didn't seem to like the Thorburg Theatre and she said the School wanted painting."

"So it does," said her mother.

"Oh, well. I suppose so, but it seemed – well, sort of cheek on her part. She's very quiet in most ways, so quiet that it embarrasses me, but then she says something blunt and I can't help feeling irritated. Then I get a conscience, because she *is* an orphan and I did mean to be nice to her. I'm so lucky – we all are. Only I think it's a case of complete incompatibility."

Her mother did not laugh at the long word and her tragic face.

"Oh, heavens, I do hope not! Because she's with us now for always. Or at least until she's old enough to go her own way."

"I hope not, too, but I'm afraid it's true. Maybe she'll get her own friends, and once we're back at the Thorburg –"

"Yes, but we can't shut her out. We must try and draw her into the family. It will take time, of course, so *don't* make up your mind."

"I'll try not. I did mean to do better."

"Well, anyway, I got front Circle seats for you and Joan and Delph for Saturday afternoon at the Thorburg, and an extra one in case Lisa wanted to go with you."

"*Les Sylphides, Peter and the Wolf* and *Graduation Ball*. Well, Joan ought to like that. Only I don't really know what she likes. She may say it's daft."

"*Did* she say that?"

"Over ballet training, I think it was. The same exercises for years. Oh, well, we'll all go and try to see that she enjoys it."

Left alone, Anne continued to frown as she brushed her sleek red hair. Oh, why did life suddenly seem less happy and interesting than usual? Why was there this feeling of nagging worry at the back of her mind? It wasn't only Joan. It was Lisa, of course. She had spoken to her on the telephone an hour ago and had once more been conscious that Lisa wasn't quite her usual self. She hadn't seemed nearly as pleased as usual to be going back to the School.

"Something's wrong," thought Anne, "and I wish she'd tell me. I hate not knowing. But oh! it will be good to get back to the Thorburg!"

The house was astir early the next morning and breakfast for the three youngest Garlands was at a quarter to eight. Joan, told that she could have hers at half-past with her uncle and aunt and Pelagia, nevertheless rose early and bathed. Lying in bed only gave her unhappy thoughts more time to take possession of her.

When she went down Anne and Delphine were wearing their green Thorburg suits and blouses, and Edward the green blazer and tie and grey trousers that were the boy's uniform. The hall was littered with satchels and neat little cases. Anne's case was green and square, with her initials on it.

Delphine had forgotten a towel, Anne had mysteriously lost her school gloves, and Edward, ignoring the feminine bustle, picked up his things and set off alone to meet a friend at Baker Street Station.

"Lisa said she'd walk over," said Anne, finding the gloves at last in the hall cupboard. "We'd better go out and see if she's coming. Stop preening, Delph. You look beautiful!"

"This green beret does rather suit me," said Delphine. "At *this* angle, do you think? But I still don't want to go to the blessed Thorburg –"

"Oh, skip it, Delph! You'll adore it." And Anne shrieked with relief to find Lisa Thorburg climbing the steps. "We're just ready. 'Bye, everyone! 'Bye, Joan! See you tonight!"

Joan watched the three away, thinking that Lisa Thorburg looked nice. But how very, very odd to be going to a ballet school, starting the day with a dancing lesson. Yet Anne looked more cheerful than she had done since Tuesday. Clearly she loved her extraordinary world.

Frowning in puzzlement, Joan went to help Rosa carry in the things for the second breakfast, and for quite a time her mind struggled to follow the would-be dancers, trying to imagine their lives.

Meanwhile, the would-be dancers themselves jostled their way into the Tube at Baker Street and strap-hung as far as Piccadilly, where they had to change for Russell Square. There were, in fact, a number of ways in which they could go to school and sometimes they varied them. They could go by Underground to St Pancras and King's Cross and change there, for instance, only that often meant even greater crowds, and they could go by bus to Euston Square, cross two busy roads and catch another one. But, whenever the weather was fine, Anne and Lisa usually managed to do the best part of the journey together.

It was a nuisance having Delphine with them, Anne thought, for it gave them no real chance to talk, but, in any case, the trains were too crowded at that hour for any sort of intimate conversation.

Crossing Russell Square they saw green-clad figures converging from all directions, and soon met a particular friend, Fernanda Vrego, a Spanish girl who had been at the Thorburg for two years. Fernanda lived with an aunt who lived in London, and flew home to Spain for the holidays, a procedure that was by no means unusual at the ballet school, where there were many foreign students. They also met a boy they all liked, Colin Corbett, and the four went on in a bunch, with Delphine, sulky and frowning at being overlooked, trailing behind.

Anne remembered her, with compunction, as they reached the steps.

"You have met Delphine before, haven't you? She's been to shows and things. And you've met her at home once or twice, of course."

Fernanda and Colin smiled at the younger girl and Fernanda said: "And now you start as a pupil? How well I remember my first day! I had almost no English and Lisa and Anne were so kind."

"We'd better find someone to be kind to Delph," Anne remarked, though privately she was of the opinion that it would be Delphine who took someone under her wing. After all, she knew many people by name and by sight and could not be counted a real stranger.

In the hall she spied a girl who had joined the school the previous term.

"Hey, Carrie! You've had a term, so you know the ropes. Will you show Delphine – my sister – the cloakrooms and her classroom and studio and everything?"

Carrie, who was ten years old and had an engaging grin, said deferentially: "Of course, Anne. How do you do, Delphine? I'd better take you to Miss Jones first. She's ticking off the new girls on her list."

"I don't *really* count as quite new, you know," Delphine said clearly. "After all, I've heard about the Thorburg since before I could walk."

Carrie looked taken aback.

"Yes, I expect so, with your mother being Mona Garland and everything. But you'd still better come to Miss Jones."

Delphine was borne off and Anne sighed.

"I only hope she doesn't put everyone's back up in the first half-hour." But then she forgot all about her sister in the sheer pleasure of being back in the familiar atmosphere, greeting friends in the cloakroom – the cloakrooms were in the basement – and in exchanging holiday gossip. The worried, faintly guilty feeling caused by her inability to get on with Joan had quite receded as she changed hastily into her practice tights and leotard, and she and Lisa set off towards the small hall-cum-theatre, where all the junior and senior students gathered briefly on the first morning of term. After a short speech by the headmistress, Miss Shane, and the reading of a few notices, the familiar round of ballet classes and school work would begin.

At the top of the cloakroom stairs they again encountered Colin, also in practice clothes. He was frowning.

"Lost something?" Anne asked cheerfully, swinging her cloak on her arm. It was far too warm to need it, but they were always supposed to put them on after ballet class.

"No. But I say! I was just trying to think, and now I remember. Guess who I've just seen?"

"Haven't the foggiest."

"Helenka Koronov."

A rush of blank dismay filled Anne and she stared at him with her mouth a little open.

"You couldn't have. She went to America."

"I'm sure it *was* Helenka, all the same. She's altered – grown much taller and plainer – and I recognized her mother. They were just disappearing with Miss Shane. Her mother used to dance with the Bolshoi, didn't she? Very striking-looking!"

"Oh, I do hope you were mistaken!" Anne cried and felt Lisa's hand on her arm. She turned and met her friend's understanding eyes and pulled a little face as they went on their way towards the hall.

"She'll have altered. Colin said she had," said Lisa.

"Not her," Anne said ruefully, still fighting deep dismay. "In looks she may have done, but I bet her character hasn't."

The only real unhappiness she had ever experienced at the Thorburg had been caused by Helenka Koronov, and, though it was all long ago, she vividly remembered the anguish of it all. Helenka had been new on the same day as Anne and Lisa, and Anne had been put to sit with her in class, though she had known by then that she and Lisa would be friends. They had already met a few times, as Johann Thorburg and Mona Garland had secretly hoped for that very thing.

Helenka and Anne, by contrast, had just never got on from the first moment and it had really been Helenka's fault. She was a precocious ten-year-old; clever, pretty and perhaps not unlike Delphine at the same age. She had set out to impress Anne and all the others in her class and had ended up by being very unpopular.

Somehow, Anne had never quite known how she and Helenka had become bitter rivals, both at dancing and at their ordinary school work, and the whole thing had come to a head during their second term, the Christmas term, when the Junior School was in a ferment over the coming Christmas Show. All knew that only a few from each class could be chosen and Anne had longed for a certain part in one of the short ballets. To her amazed delight she had been given the part and Helenka had been furious. She had said a great many unforgivable things about Anne only being chosen because her mother was Mona Garland and her family were friends with Johann Thorburg, and Anne, who had not then learned to control a fiery temper, had flown at Helenka. They had had an undignified fight, during which Helenka had fallen and cut her head badly on a desk. The whole thing had come out into the open, and there had been a dreadful row.

Anne had lost the part as a punishment and the rest of the term had been very unhappy for both of them. It had mattered little to Anne that opinion had definitely been on her side. She had felt ashamed and hurt, and it had been very bitter indeed to have to watch the Christmas Show from the audience. She and Helenka had never spoken to each other again, and Anne had been glad when Christmas came, with a break from the Thorburg.

Her relief had been enormous when Helenka had not reappeared after Christmas and she had learned that the three Koronovs had gone to live in New York. Since then there had been no more trouble of any kind and Anne had gone her happy way, with many friends.

But if Helenka had really come back …

And Helenka had. Most of the school was already assembled when a girl came into the hall with Miss Jones. She had already changed into practice clothes and she slipped into the place indicated, in the same row as Anne.

One glimpse was enough, though she had certainly changed very much. Gone was the dazzlingly pretty, dark-haired little girl, with the pert, self-satisfied expression. In her place was a much taller, thinner girl, with a pale, almost tragic face and her dark hair in a pony-tail.

Anne thought vaguely that she looked far more Russian than she had in the past. The sight of her old rival stirred up so many uncomfortable memories that she hastily shrank back into her seat and shut out the sight of Helenka. Oh, how hatefully difficult life was being! It was almost as though fate was suddenly against her.

"I shall keep out of her way," she muttered to Lisa, who nodded.

"Perhaps it would be best. But she's to be in our class, you see. She's the same age. It's inevitable."

"Didn't your father say anything about her?"

"No. Of course he has very little to do with the Juniors. It's all Miss Shane and Miss Cargli." Miss Cargli was the principal ballet mistress of the School. "You see, she probably wasn't auditioned as she was here before. She may just have come with recommendations from the New York school she was at. Oh, Anne, I'm awfully sorry!"

"So am I," Anne said ruefully. "But we're older now and more sensible and it's a big class. I shall just ignore her."

And, when she and Helenka met face to face on arrival at the studio, she looked blankly at the Russian girl and passed on to join Fernanda over by the *barre*. The boys had separate ballet classes, and so were not present.

Helenka had stopped abruptly, as though she were going to speak, but she was left staring after Anne.

Fernanda, who was very observant, looked surprised.

"Who is that? That new girl? She looked as though she knew you, but you swept past just like a duchess."

"My old enemy," Anne said lightly, though she felt heavy-hearted.

"You are not the sort to have enemies. Don't be silly!"

"Not now. I didn't ever think it was my fault then. Tell you later." And Anne began to warm up, glad to feel the comfort of the familiar movements and the smoothness of the *barre* under her hands.

But, when the class started, she was startled to hear Lisa being pulled up for wrong positions and careless movements in the centre practice. Lisa, who was hardly ever in trouble, was a good, reliable dancer, with few of the troublesome faults often pointed out and corrected in the others.

"But, Lisa dear, haven't you been practising in the holidays?"

"Oh, yes, Miss Tindall. Sometimes."

" 'Sometimes' isn't enough. I'm sure your father can't have known."

"No-o, Miss Tindall."

"Well, let me see that *enchaînement* again."

After the class they changed hastily back into their ordinary clothes, and the period until break was spent making time-tables and receiving new books. Helenka was put to sit with another new girl at the opposite end of the classroom, but Anne caught many curious glances and knew that others were remembering the old affair.

"I won't let her bother me. I'll just keep on ignoring her," she thought, but the pleasure of the day was spoilt.

There was a canteen at the Thorburg where all those who wished could get a meal in the middle of the day, and the Garlands usually stayed. It was too far for them to go home and back again in the time. Anne sat at a small table with Lisa, Fernanda, Colin and another boy and they were a merry group on the whole; only Lisa sat almost in silence, with a slight frown on her expressive face.

"Are you worrying about getting pulled up by Miss

Tindall?" Anne whispered, and was startled by the look in her friend's eyes.

"No, why should I be?"

'Well, but – but – I just thought – *I* should mind. Though you weren't the only one by a long way."

"I deliberately didn't practise. I didn't *want* to. You see –"

"Please, Anne!" cried an urgent voice at her elbow and she spun round to see the younger girl called Carrie Gray.

"Anne, do please come!"

"Why? What is it? Delphine?" Anne glanced about and saw that most of the Juniors and many of the others had gone. She and her friends had been lingering over milky coffee.

"Yes. Please, Anne, she's dancing in the Big Studio, and I'm so scared that one of the Seniors or staff will see her. They're all in there – our class. She *made* them go in."

Anne leaped up. Was there no end to her present worries?

"But they know they aren't allowed in the Big Studio. The Seniors might catch them at any minute. They're not all new. Haven't they any sense, even if Delph hasn't?"

"I – I don't know, Anne." Carrie's voice was humble and apologetic.

Anne dashed off along the corridor, up the stairs and gently opened the door of the Big Studio, which was regarded as being entirely reserved for the most important senior students. At the other end of the room was a group of Juniors, clustered close together and staring in rather a mesmerized way at Delphine, who, in her short pleated skirt and green blouse, was dancing.

"There!" Delphine cried triumphantly. "That was my own choreography, too. The Thorburg may not think much of me, but one day you'll be able to say that you saw the future Pavlova, and think how honoured you'll feel."

"Think how jolly small *you'd* have felt if someone important had caught you in here!" Anne said smartly from the background. "Really, Delph, how can you be so silly? Hop off at once, the lot of you!"

Delphine glared, but her contemporaries began to fade hastily away. Anne heard one of them mutter: "That Delphine's got too much of an opinion of herself, even if her mother *is* Mona Garland!"

"Did you hypnotize them, or what?" she asked, when she and her sister were alone. "You know that the Big Studio's kept for the Seniors. And you'll be so unpopular, anyway, if you show off."

"I told them I had something very special to show them," Delphine said complacently. "And this was the only private place."

"Special? Your dancing?"

"Why not?" asked Delphine, with rather an engaging grin. "And, after all, if I do turn into a future Pavlova they will have seen me make up a dance when I was just turned ten."

Anne gave her a shove and shut the door firmly behind them.

"There's the bell. Fly upstairs or you'll be late for your next lesson."

Making her own way to her classroom on the second floor she remembered, with disquiet, Lisa's strange words: "I didn't *want* to practise!" Oh, what had come over Lisa? What had come over life? And when would things go comfortably back to normal?

Chapter Six
Saturday Matinée

Meanwhile, Joan – left alone at Moone Crescent while everyone else was occupied – took Bonne-Bouche for a walk and for the first time really looked at the part of London to which she had come. She walked very slowly in the warm sunshine, staring with awe and a slowly dawning pleasure at the vast, elegant cream terraces, so different from anything she had seen in her native Lancashire.

She turned down Sussex Place, walking still more slowly and wondering what kind of people lived there, and peeped rather shyly into the cobbled seclusion of Sussex Mews. Then she crossed the road and entered the park and wandered over to the little lake beside the big one, where children were happily paddling canoes or bumping about in small boats.

Looking back, she could still see one of the vast terraces through the trees, its high domes sharp against the very blue sky, and she thought in amazement: "I'm here – in London! I'm going to live here."

Thoughts of her recent loss followed quickly and the realization that, though she was living in London, she in no way belonged there. The Garlands didn't want her, that was certain, and she would never understand their world.

She walked on, trying hard to control her face, but feeling tears surging to the surface. A kindly-looking nanny, pushing a smart pram, glanced at her curiously – a shabby, sad-looking girl with a lively black poodle on an ornate red lead – and Joan, seeing the look, turned and stared fiercely at the water-fowl.

Half an hour after she had returned to Moone Crescent, when she was helping Rosa to clean the silver and listening to stories of the high Alpine village, Mona Garland came home. She swept Joan away from the kitchen, kindly but firmly.

"Come on, dear. We haven't too much time. We'll go down to Debenhams in a taxi. The car is more of a nuisance than anything else, parking's so difficult. No, you won't need a coat, but put on a hat and gloves."

"I've only got my old gloves and – and my school beret."

Mona Garland glanced at the wholly miserable and defiant face and said gently: "We'll get you everything you need. Not perhaps today, but soon. And perhaps you don't need a hat. Your hair's very pretty."

She and Joan were whirled away to Oxford Street and Joan shrank as they entered the big shop. It felt terrible – and yet in a way exciting and satisfying – to be with someone as smart and assured as her aunt. People seemed literally to spring to serve them, and in no time at all, with scarcely a chance to be ashamed of her shabby underclothes, Joan had a pleated skirt, several pretty blouses, two cardigans and a dress made of smart checked material, very well cut and with a broad leather belt.

Joan did venture to ask: "Oughtn't I to have dark things? Grey, perhaps?" But her aunt shook her head.

"You're too young to wear mourning, you know, and all these pretty colours do suit you. Now we'll get you a coat and some sort of attractive beret, and gloves and a new handbag. I'm afraid the coat will be too warm for now, but the weather will soon turn colder now that September's getting on."

And Joan found herself with a dark turquoise-blue coat, the sort of smooth leather gloves that she had never owned in her life, and a beautiful little shoulder-bag, with a zip-pocket and a comb, looking-glass and purse. Then they bought some shoes.

"For best," said Mona Garland, smiling so warmly that Joan once more swallowed her protests. She was horrified by the amount of money that was being spent, but clearly her aunt was enjoying herself and what was the good of arguing? At least she might be able to hold her own better when she was well-dressed.

She was then hurried off to a late lunch, laden with parcels.

"We'll just have a quick meal and then dash off to the shop that does the uniform for the Scott-Smithson School."

"Oh, please don't spend any more!" Joan begged gruffly, toying with her cold ham and salad.

"Now look, my dear! There's nothing to worry about, and everything will last you for years." Though really it wasn't true, with the child clearly growing so fast. But her aunt had been secretly delighted to see the difference to Joan when she wore the checked dress. It had softened her angles and made her look quite pretty.

The uniform suit, big coat, cap and raincoat were all in very dark red and the blouses were cream. The coat and raincoat had to be left to be altered, but they returned in a taxi carrying everything else and Joan was sent upstairs to put on the new dress and shoes.

"Our appointment is at four, so we haven't much time. But it isn't far. Just in Dorset Square."

Joan was terrified by the thought of facing yet another strange person – and a headmistress, too. By then she had a headache and felt more bewildered than ever. But she was pleased with her appearance when she was ready and the sight gave her a little confidence.

This time they set off on foot and were soon walking down Gloucester Place towards Dorset Square. Joan walked in awkward silence, so Mona Garland took the opportunity to talk about the neighbourhood.

"The tall building you see in the Marylebone Road is the Marylebone Town Hall. And what do you think of our local skyscraper?"

They were now on the north-east corner of Dorset Square and Joan stared at the big square block, the green glass shining in the sun, that showed above the houses opposite.

"It's fine, but not really a skyscraper, is it? They'd laugh at it in New York."

It was then that Mona Garland forgot caution and asked, with perhaps some condescension in her tone: "And what do you know about New York?"

Joan bristled, for it was so clear that these people thought she knew nothing, and it hurt her northern pride.

"Quite a lot, actually. One of Mother's friends had lived in New York for three years and she often showed us photographs and told us about the Empire State Building and the RCA Building and all the others. Why, the Empire State has over a hundred storeys. Just because people live in Rochdale or Wardle, or in lonely houses on the hills, it doesn't mean that they haven't been anywhere. Besides, I've often seen New York in films."

"And now I've been rude," she thought wretchedly. "Rude to a famous ballerina, and she *is* trying to be kind."

She was startled when her aunt said: "Yes, I'm sorry. We do tend to think of the North as darkest England. It's dreadful of us, and maybe you can teach us a lot. I really mean it, too. Now here we are at the school. Don't be scared. Miss Smithson is very nice. I met her once and have spoken to her on the telephone."

All the same, the interview was an ordeal for Joan and she shrank into her shell and said very little. The school, not unlike the Thorburg, was in two converted houses, and it seemed very small after the Grammar School. But there was an artroom on the top floor, a gym and various other special rooms, and the classrooms at the front were filled with afternoon sunshine.

Perhaps to impress Mona Garland, Miss Smithson referred several times to some of her more important pupils, and Joan thought in angry despair that it was clearly a snobby place and that she would be even more hopelessly out of things than she was in the Garland household. The thought that perhaps she might have a certain value because she was the niece of a ballerina brought her pride up in arms.

"I won't tell the girls," she told herself, as they all three stood in the entrance hall at the end of the interview. "They'll find out, I suppose, but I won't mention it. They can like me for myself or not at all."

"Well, goodbye for the present, Joan dear," Miss Smithson said graciously. "But I'll see you at nine o'clock on Tuesday morning. And I hope you'll be very happy with us."

Out in the square again, Mona Garland glanced at the neat gardens in the centre.

"I always like this square. The houses are all of the same period and symmetrical, and the garden is so well kept. I believe that the Scott-Smithson Seniors are allowed to have the key of the gate and walk in the garden sometimes. One day you will, too."

But Joan couldn't imagine ever being a Senior in the Scott-Smithson School. She doubted if she would survive until the end of the following week.

To Joan, used to a very quiet life at home, the house

seemed to be in a turmoil after their return. Pelagia was lying on the sofa in the living-room, wearing black jeans, a red sweater (fancy red with such flaming hair, thought Joan, who had not realized that many red-heads now considered it exciting to wear scarlet or shocking pink), and with her hair out of its usual smooth knot and tied back with what looked like an old boot-lace. On the record-player at her side was a record of the New World Symphony, and the violent end of the first movement poured over her.

Mr Garland was on the telephone in his little study, with the door partly open, and his voice, unusually loud, was roaring about something to do with lost orchestral parts. Annali and Rosa had the radio on in the kitchen and the sound of a popular tune came faintly through when Pelagia abruptly turned off the New World in the middle of the second movement.

Delphine, the first to arrive home from school, arrived with a crash, slamming the front door, dropping her case and shrieking for her mother.

"Mother! Mother! Here I am and simply starving!"

"But where's Anne?" Mona Garland asked, appearing from the drawing-room. "Did you come alone? You know it's a long way and starting to get busy at this time. I told Anne –"

"I know, but I came with another new girl who lives just off Baker Street. Anne and Lisa don't want me."

Her mother didn't argue. So long as Delphine had company that was probably enough. She was very independent and was well accustomed to going about London alone.

"And how did you get on?"

"Oh, I didn't think much of it."

"Not think much of it? But –"

"Well, why should I? I'm sick of Thorburg worship. It's a perfectly ordinary place. We had a ballet class and got given time-tables and books and I was put to sit with a girl called Carrie Gray, but I was bored with her and told Miss Grant – that's my form mistress – that really I preferred my own company, as there were some empty desks. The new ones are an awfully stuffy lot, too; so over-awed to find themselves there and scared to say boo. I thought I might as well let them know what was what, so I made up a dance and they all watched, and Anne was mad because we were in the Big Studio. What is it? A holy temple, or what? And this afternoon Miss Grant said I was the rudest new girl she ever remembered and I'd better watch my step."

"Good heavens!" said Mona Garland, rather faintly. "You'd better not let your father hear you. It sounds like quite a day."

Delphine gave her mother an endearing grin.

"I mean to make my mark. The other new ones don't know what to make of me, and neither does that Carrie, but they don't quite hate me. But you'll never know what harm it did to my ego being turned down in the first place."

"It'll harm it a lot more, my child, if you're chucked out. You really must behave."

"They'd never chuck out Mona Garland's daughter."

"Don't be too sure, and if you are you'll be in the worst trouble you've ever known. This house will be too hot to hold you. Now go and wash. You look like a sweep, and must you wear your beret like that?"

"I thought it looked rather dashing. I do think Edward's stuck up. He practically ignored me. There he was in Russell Square with a lot of other boys and he didn't introduce me to one of them."

"They're more than four years older and think themselves pretty important. You're small fry."

"Wow!" said Delphine and shot up the stairs, past the astonished Joan, who had been listening, without quite meaning to, on the landing.

Edward arrived next, also with something of a crash, and Anne followed close behind, more quietly.

The upper part of the house was then filled with the sound of voices, running water and drawers opening and shutting. After that everyone flew down for the meal, which was at five-thirty for everybody, except for Mona Garland herself, who, not dancing that night, was going out to dinner.

Joan entered the room last, shy and self-conscious in her new dress, and it was Delphine who cried: "Oh, I say! How smashing! Don't you look smart? Did you get a lot of things?"

"Did you see your new school?" Anne added, with a visible effort. She looked pale and thoughtful and not at all as though she had had a happy day.

But after that no one took much notice of Joan, and the talk ranged over what she was beginning to think of as "the eternal subjects". Pelagia chattered on about the coming tour and about costumes and what various people had said, Edward was apparently upset because one of the boys in his class had had an accident and wouldn't be able to dance all term, and Delphine tried to make herself heard and looked sulky when she failed.

"What's the matter, Anne?" her mother asked presently. She was sitting with them, having a cup of coffee, as it was too early to dress.

"Nothing."

"There must be something. Or have you got a headache?"

"Yes, I have a bit. It's just that – well, I'm worried about Lisa."

The whole family fell silent and surveyed her curiously.

"What's the matter with Lisa?" asked her father.

"I don't know. That's just it. She started to say something, but she wouldn't say any more. I tried all the way home. I've tried for weeks."

"Her father said something about being worried about her," said Mona Garland, frowning. "There must be something if you've noticed it, too."

"Oh, it sticks out a mile that she's miserable. I wish I knew why. And Helenka Koronov is back again."

There was silence until Delphine asked: "Who on earth is she?"

"You wouldn't know. It was years ago. She got me into trouble. Or we got each other."

"That unfortunate business!" said Edwin Garland, looking anxious. "When you lost the part and there was a row? I thought she went to New York. I got the impression that most people were glad, though she was a promising child for her age."

"Well, she's back and looking like someone out of Chekov. Quite different. But it made me remember –"

"Three years can make a lot of difference. You're both older and more sensible."

"She was rather a little twerp," said Pelagia. "I remember her well. She used to cheek the Seniors, and she had some ballet shoes that used to belong to Ulanova that she was always flaunting."

"That's the one," Anne agreed sadly. "Now she's in my class again."

"Well, it's a big enough class, only don't fight if one of you gets a good part in the Christmas show."

"Never again. I shouldn't say a word if she danced her Rose Adagio. But what ought I to do? I just ignored her."

"Perhaps that's best," said Pelagia, from the lofty heights of one who had left school far behind.

"But it's not easy and it makes me feel uncomfortable. Oh, I do think that life is difficult!"

Joan endorsed the words, though for very different reasons. She, too, had a headache, and a heartache as well, and the always partly incomprehensible conversation – and so much of it – left her feeling an utter outsider. She escaped as soon as she could, and taking *Jane Eyre* from one of the bookcases, went up to her own room, flung herself on the bed, and read herself into oblivion.

By Saturday afternoon Joan could scarcely believe that it was still barely a week since her old life had finished. Much less than a week since she had sat high on the hill above Watergrove. Her initial feeling that she would never fit into the Garland household was hardening into a grim, silent withdrawal. Much that she had seen and heard she told herself that she despised, but it was not really true. In her heart she was fascinated. But the only thing that was really clear was that she was different, and her rather stern pride made her resolve that she would keep herself apart and not bother any of them.

The only person in the whole household with whom she felt at ease was Rosa, the dumpy, young Swiss girl who was also suffering acute pangs of homesickness. Rosa spoke English with some difficulty, but they managed to understand each other well enough, and Joan's most relaxed moments were when she was helping Rosa about the house. For Joan liked housework and enjoyed dusting and polishing all the lovely ornaments.

"At home we hadn't anything like this," she said, carefully handling a big Italian bowl.

"We have not, no," Rosa agreed. "Ver' plain, old chalet where I live and things useful not – not –"

"Not beautiful or decorative? I know. I like beautiful things. But none of these are old. I never thought I liked very modern things before. But most of their things have a – a lovely line."

That was incomprehensible to Rosa, but even so they understood each other sufficiently for their relationship to be a comfort.

On Friday afternoon Joan's box arrived, and she saw, with pain and some anger, that her possessions looked even older and shabbier than she remembered. Even her pictures were in cheap little frames. But she put up two prints and felt better having them there.

Anne, looking in on her return from school, to ask rather awkwardly how she had got on, cried: "Oh, Lowry! I like that one. It's in the Tate. I've seen it."

"It's called *The Pond*. Could I – see the real one?"

"Oh, why not? Any time. Down on Millbank."

Joan didn't know where Millbank was, but resolved to find out. The little Lowry, with its innumerable minute figures and crowding houses, was a picture of her native county. It seemed odd that Anne should like it, when she so clearly saw the North as ugly and unimportant.

"Do you – like art?"

Anne nodded, mopping her still damp face with the towel she carried. It was one of the household rules that everyone should wash and tidy up after school.

"Oh, yes. Degas, of course, is my favourite. But I love the French Impressionists and people like Duffy and Marquet and Bernard Buffet. It's very important for us. We often get taken to exhibitions."

"But why? Ballet is just movement –"

"Oh, it's not. You'll see tomorrow. It's everything. Art and music and movement – and the story, of course, when there is one. We have such a lot to learn. We learn music and painting, but, though I love art, I'm quite hopeless. I draw and paint like a four-year-old. I'm the art mistress's despair."

And Joan did not bother to say that she had won prizes for art and had once had a picture shown all over the country in a Children's Art Exhibition.

But she felt a faint feeling of curiosity and excitement at the thought of seeing ballet, especially the one called *Les*

Sylphides that she had seen on television and that was danced to heavenly Chopin music.

A further shopping expedition on Friday morning had provided her with new underwear, pyjamas, a dressing-gown and two pretty dresses suitable for the theatre. She put on the red and white one after an early lunch on Saturday.

Lisa, to Anne's silent despair and puzzlement, had made some excuse not to go to the Thorburg Theatre with them, and Fernanda was to go instead, meeting Anne, Delphine and Joan in Kingsway.

Joan was very silent in the train, but as they came out of the Tube station she suddenly darted over to a sweet kiosk and bought a small box of chocolates. She had been given some pocket-money that morning and had already had several pounds forced on her by kindly Mrs Thwaite.

Anne, she thought, looked rather odd when she returned, and Delphine was frankly staring.

"Why have you got chocolates?"

At Delphine's tone Joan bristled, though she was at a loss to understand.

"Well, we're going to the theatre. People always have chocolates at the theatre."

"People who go twice a year for a nice outing," Delphine said. "Rustling their beastly paper and saying, 'Here's a nice soft one, dear!' *just* at the quietest moment."

Joan stood stock-still in the middle of the crowded pavement, her face white and the chocolates clasped to her chest.

"I think you're the beastliest, smuggest child I've ever met! You're all smug, smug, smug! I don't understand you at all. I hate you!"

Anne, appalled, both because Joan was so upset and because people were staring, took her arm and urged her towards the Thorburg.

"We'll eat them in the interval and thank you very much, Joan. Delph *was* smug, but I'm sorry you think we all are. You see, we really don't go to the theatre just for a nice night out. We go because it's – it's life. Just a part of life. And we really do rather hate people who have to eat all through the most moving and exciting parts. Cellophane on sweets is the worst stuff in the world, and some people are dreadful. Not long ago we sat in front of some people who just never stopped, and in the end Edward said quite loudly that it would be fish and chips next, as they must be starving. That was rude of him, I suppose, but all the things people find to eat is one of our family jokes, potato crisps and peanuts. Johann Thorburg won't have *them*. He once said they were a sin against the theatre." She had talked on, rather frantically, but Joan still looked grim and suddenly tossed the box into a litter bin.

"I'll leave it there, then."

"You shouldn't have done that. Oh, dear! I'm sorry! And here's Fernanda, so we'd better not say any more."

Fernanda was introduced to Joan, who did her best to smile and look natural, but she was still seething as they climbed the red-carpeted stairs to the Circle. Anne bought programmes for all of them – in Joan's experience one programme did for everyone, but she had heard the Garlands speak of their collections of theatre programmes – and they took their seats in the centre of the front row.

Fortunately, perhaps, the curtain would go up in five minutes' time, and the other three immediately buried their noses in their programmes, noting who was dancing each role and making comments and comparisons.

"Barbary Brown is dancing the Prelude in *Les Sylphides*, you see," Anne said to Joan. "And Marya Jessop the Mazurka, and Shelagh Sullavan the Waltz. That's a chance for Shelagh. She's never danced it before. People nearly always get solo parts at matinées first. Watch the girl who is the Duck in *Peter*. She's one of Pelagia's friends. You may meet her one day."

"And Pelagia –?" Joan gazed at the programme, trying to take things in.

"There, just in the *corps de ballet* in *Les Sylphides*. And one of the younger schoolgirls in *Graduation Ball*."

By the time that the house-lights went down and the first notes of the Chopin music began to steal through the theatre, Joan was a little soothed. It was, after all, exciting to be in a theatre, and she was aware of a sharp, almost painful curiosity over the dancing she was going to see. But the lovely music went straight to her heart and brought a stab of sudden and almost unbearable pain that had been her companion on and off for a week.

"If I cry," she thought desperately, "they'll think – they'll be ashamed of me. I *mustn't* cry!"

Then the curtains slid quietly apart, revealing the blue-lit stage, with its backcloth of trees and the grouped white figures of the dancers, and Joan sank down into a sort of incredulous enchantment. For it wasn't, really, anything like the television performance, which had been on a very small screen in a living-room, where her friend had talked a little and there had been no chance to sink into complete oblivion.

For quite a long time she was lost, her body moving very slightly to the rhythm of the music, her whole being absorbed by the patterns made by the *corps de ballet* and by the leaping, airy movements of the solo dancers. It was not real; it was a magic thing, as divorced from real life as a fairy story. And then she recognized Pelagia among all those young girls in soft, filmy white dresses, with wreaths in their hair: Pelagia, with her smooth red hair marking her out from the rest, though only a little of it showed; Pelagia with a remote, entranced expression. And it seemed utterly fantastic that this was the girl of whom she was more than a little afraid: the oldest Garland, who lay about in jeans and tight sweaters, playing loud music and sometimes talking in wild excitement about the coming tour.

This was the thing to which they all gave their lives. That was her own uncle down there in the orchestra pit, waving his baton with such authority. This was the thing that even little Delphine was learning to do: this lovely, dreamlike dancing that was born of endless hours at the *barre*; of sore toes and sweat-stained practice clothes, of hope and fear. For even a few days in the Garland household, listening to their endless talk, had taught Joan that there was fear; fear of not being good enough, of not being chosen, of growing too tall, of injury.

Oh, but it was lovely! She clasped her hot hands and stared, tense all over in her complete concentration. It was beautiful, but it wasn't – couldn't be – the whole of life. And yet all the Garlands thought that it was.

The fall of the curtain found her shaken and unwilling to face the lights. But luckily no one said anything to her at first. They were discussing the technical points, arguing about the girl called Shelagh, saying things about *grands jetés* and *pas de bourrée* that were quite definitely Greek to Joan.

"Did you like it, Joan?" Anne asked at last.

"Oh, yes. I – I did. They looked – I found it hard to remember that they're real."

"It's those soulful expressions," Anne said lightly. "Pel often said at first that it was one of the hardest things to do – to look like that when holding a position for so long in a piercing draught. Or if you think you're going to sneeze or hiccup. It must get frightfully boring for the *corps*, poor dears, and some of them won't ever dance the solo roles. They haven't even got that to look forward to, though I suppose most of them hope."

Joan turned to look at Anne.

"I'll never understand! You know it from the inside. Are you frightfully bored watching it, then?"

"Oh, no, never, though I've seen *Sylphides* more than most. All companies do it. Sometimes I even forget everything but the – the whole atmosphere, as it were. Of course you'll find the two other ballets very different." She was pleased, and relieved, to find that at least her cousin wasn't calling it "proper daft".

And Joan certainly did find *Peter and the Wolf* very different from *Les Sylphides*. Gone was the soft, blue-lit enchantment and in its place was a livelier, more colourful affair. A real fairy tale, with a commentator, and the audience often laughed.

Graduation Ball, to Strauss's music, was funny too, and quite gone was Pelagia's "other world" expression. She was just a young and rather naughty schoolgirl enjoying her first ball. But even here there were things that brought sharp pleasure and an awareness of what technical brilliance might mean. There was jazz dancing in the *divertissement*, put on for the entertainment of schoolgirls and cadets.

It was all fascinating and she knew that she would want to see other ballets. One thing she had certainly learned, that ballet was very different from a Christmas pantomime, and that she heartily agreed with her cousins that eating chocolates would be – well, awful! Especially in *Les Sylphides*.

But the moment they emerged from the theatre she felt stiff, shy and out of things again. She had had a glimpse of the Garland world, but it was not, could never be, her own. And she looked at the London streets, remembering, with terrible homesickness, the empty hills of home.

Chapter Seven

A Tragedy for Pelagia

On Sunday morning it transpired that there was to be another expedition so that Joan could get to know London – this time to the Tower. Delphine had never been and Anne and Edward only once.

"I'm afraid that Londoners just don't see their own city," Mona Garland said, noting Joan's surprised face.

"We'll all go," said Pelagia unexpectedly. "It'll be a terrible scrum, being Sunday and such fine weather, but let's go and join the mob."

"Are the boats still running?" Edward asked.

"Oh, I expect so. Yes, let's go from Westminster Pier. It will give Joan a real chance to see the river. Far more fun than Tube or bus."

Pelagia was back in her bootlace and jeans, and ever since the previous afternoon Joan had been regarding her with a mixture of awe and curiosity. It seemed so very strange to be a sylphide one minute, an old-fashioned schoolgirl the next, dancing so gaily with a cadet, and then back to reality.

"If – if you don't want to bother I expect I could go by myself."

"But we do want to bother," Anne said, as warmly as she

could. She was still worried about Lisa and Helenka, and not at all looking forward to Monday morning and the return to the Thorburg, but something had to be done to make Joan feel at home, and so long as Pelagia, Edward and Delphine went, too ... "You'll like the ravens and the Crown Jewels – though there's sure to be a queue for those – and the White Tower and the water-gates. Do you like history?"

"Yes," Joan said baldly. She had always loved it and other times were very real to her, especially the Tudor period.

"Then you'll be soaked in it, but we'd better go back some time in the winter, when there aren't so many people."

Before lunch Pelagia disappeared, to appear again wearing a smart green dress and pretty high-heeled shoes. Her hair was once more in its smooth knot, and she wore little silver ear-rings.

"If I'm in charge of the party I thought I'd better do you credit," she said, fending off the jeers and comments of her outspoken family.

"Jolly good idea!" said Edward, who, like most males, even fourteen-year-old ones, was sensitive about women's dress. "But you'll never cope with all those cobbles and narrow steps with those heels."

"They're not all that high and they're my only really respectable shoes. I've been waiting to get some in Paris. Glad you're pleased," said Pelagia calmly.

"But it sets a high standard for the rest of us. Do we have to dress up like a row of dogs' dinners just to go to the Tower?" Anne grumbled.

"No need to be a dog's dinner. You generally look nice, anyway."

Urged on by all this, Joan washed and the party set off cheerfully, with Joan the most silent member of it.

They went to Westminster by bus, and by the river the scene was very bright and crowded.

"Soon it'll be winter," said Anne, with a sigh, "and I'd so much sooner have summer. Soon we'll be wearing macs and gum boots and battling our way across Russell Square in floods of rain."

"But there are compensations," said Edward. "Skating, and Christmas, and the Christmas Show."

"You know we hardly ever dare to skate because of sprained ankles, and the show causes me far more agony than pleasure."

"It doesn't once you're chosen. Look! Dive into that queue. It's the shortest. We can't stand all afternoon waiting for a boat. It wasn't such a good idea, after all."

But they were able to board a boat without too much delay and were soon off down the river towards Waterloo Bridge.

"That's County Hall," Anne pointed out. "And the Royal Festival Hall, of course. You saw both as we walked along the Embankment. And there's old Scotland Yard ... and the Savoy Hotel along there – and Somerset House beyond the Bridge.

"Waterloo Station is over there, and the National Theatre is also on the right. You'll have to go there. Do you like Shakespeare?"

"Yes," said Joan. She did indeed like Shakespeare, but refrained from remarking that she had only ever seen one, and that had been *Julius Caesar* done by one of the local schools. She moved away from her cousins.

"She's so dreadfully quiet," Anne sighed to Pelagia. "Do you think she enjoys anything? I feel all the time that she doesn't like or approve of us."

"She thinks we're pretty odd."

"But we're not, are we?"

"I wouldn't know. We're not, in our narrow little world."

"Edward said that. Something like it. I still think it's her world that's narrow. Fancy never having seen London! It seems fantastic."

"A good proportion of the population haven't, I suppose," Pelagia remarked.

"Someone ought to start a Free Holidays in London fund then," said Anne, and meant it.

Joan had, in fact, almost deliberately cut herself off from them. She was secretly enchanted with the London scene, and, as they approached the Tower, she was completely absorbed in remembering all the people who had been taken by water to that vast, grim building. So many of them had entered never to emerge into the open air again, except perhaps, to cross Tower Green to the scaffold. Many of them had spent years as prisoners there and had died in some dark, cold tower.

Catherine Howard, Anne Boleyn, Lady Jane Grey ... all those women had died within the Tower of London. Joan had once won a prize for an essay on Lady Jane Grey and it was strange to see the Tower in reality, rearing up against the smoothly blue September sky. She scarcely even noticed the noisy, cheerful crowds as the boat was tied up and they stepped ashore.

To the Tower ... Not as a schoolgirl on a bright September afternoon, paying at the ticket booth. Lady Jane Grey had gone as a young and frightened girl, who had got caught up, unwittingly, in matters of state.

"Come on, Joan. We'd better not lose you," said Pelagia.

Joan rather wanted to lose them. She said with sudden definiteness: "I won't be lost. I'll just be looking at things by myself and I'll meet you at the gate in – in about an hour and a half, shall I?"

"Well, perhaps. But come with us now."

The smooth turf, the ravens, the Yeoman Warders in their historic costumes, the ancient towers rising on every side ... even with crowds of people and shouting children it was easy for Joan, standing by the site of the scaffold, to slip back and back, remembering the old pain and terror of others and somehow, in the process, forgetting her own comparatively new pain.

The others wandered away, but she caught up with them again in the White Tower, feeling that perhaps she had better, after all, remain with them, for the expedition had been for her. They queued to see the Crown Jewels, and Joan was impressed, but not moved as she was by her own reconstruction of scenes long past.

When she thought about it, it made her self-conscious to be with the Garlands, for there was no doubt that people stared. They looked so conspicuous, those four confident red-heads, but she realized that Delphine was the only one who was aware of the interest they caused. Delphine could clearly not refrain from showing off; her voice was always a little too loud, her smiles and gestures a little too obvious. Once Edward said: "Shut up, for heaven's sake! You'll have people staring."

"I don't care. Why shouldn't they look at us? I like to be noticed."

"That's obvious," her brother retorted coldly.

"I don't see why it should be a sin. Really, brothers can be horrible!"

"Oh, shut up! Let's go up here."

They climbed the narrow, uneven steps without mishap, but coming down someone suddenly jostled Pelagia and she fell down the last four or five steps, landing in an awkward heap, with her handbag some distance away.

Consternation immediately reigned and her family rushed to Pelagia's side. But it was a good-looking young man, whom Joan had vaguely noticed following them, who was beside her first.

"Oh, dear! Are you hurt? No, don't move too quickly. You came an awful cropper –"

"These wretched shoes!" said Pelagia faintly. She was very white and her green eyes looked enormous in her suddenly sharpened face.

"That woman who barged into you – she never even looked round or apologized. What have you done?"

"Is it your ankle? Oh, Pel!" Anne cried.

"I expect it's just twisted or strained. I'll be all right in a minute." Pelagia, with the young man's help, levered herself up on to the bottom step and sat there trying to flex her right foot. People, seeing that she was not alone, began to pass by. The Garlands and Joan stood helplessly near her.

"A taxi –" said Edward.

"But it will cost a fortune – all the way home!" said Anne anxiously.

"Can't be helped. Her ankle's more than strained. It's swelling already."

"Yes, b-better be a taxi," said Pelagia, with chattering teeth.

"I'll help, if you get on her other side," the young man said to Edward. Clearly he had no intention of leaving Pelagia's side yet.

Edward agreed and between them they got Pelagia to her feet and, half-carrying her, made their slow way to the exit. Anne, Delphine and Joan followed, awed and dismayed.

"The tour," Anne said. "Oh, Pel, the tour!"

"I thought of it as I was falling," said Pelagia, through stiff lips.

"What tour?" asked the young man.

"Pelagia's a ballet dancer. With the Thorburg. She's going on a long Continental tour a week on Friday," Anne explained.

"Oh!" said the young man, who had been following Pelagia in fascinated admiration ever since he first spied her on Tower Green. He was really very good-looking indeed, with crisp fair hair, an intelligent face and an attractive voice. "That *is* hard luck!"

"But don't let us keep you," said Pelagia, who rather thought she might be sick at any moment.

"Oh, it's quite all right. I brought my young nephew and niece and I think they've gone back to have another look inside the White Tower. They'll be OK. I don't suppose there'll be many taxis down here –"

"I'll go and find one," said Edward, as they reached the exit and eased Pelagia on to a low wall.

"Oh, Pel, those shoes – Oh, Pel, I'm so sorry!" Anne wailed.

"It may not be anything much," said Pelagia, who was secretly convinced that her ankle was broken. Pain and despair made her look so like a martyred saint that the young man was nearly heartbroken himself.

Edward came back riding on the step of a taxi and Pelagia was tenderly helped in. The others all followed and the young man asked: "Where shall I tell the driver to go?"

"I told him, 21 Moone Crescent," said Edward. "And thank you very much for your help."

"It was nothing. I hope that ankle isn't too bad," said their new acquaintance, and the taxi sped away, leaving him staring after it, with the cheerful Sunday crowds all around him.

The long drive back to Moone Crescent was a dismal one and Joan felt horribly guilty. If it hadn't been for her Pelagia would never have been climbing uneven steps in the Tower of London.

But Edward was wholly blaming Pelagia's footwear.

"I told you those shoes were ridiculous for going round the Tower. If you'd worn flat sandals –"

"If – if – if –" Pelagia retorted crossly. "I think I'm going to be sick! Oh, well, hang on a minute. I can't get out and be sick here. No, perhaps I'm not, after all."

By the time they arrived home the ankle was terribly swollen and discoloured and she more or less had to be carried into the house. Annali and Rosa appeared with cries of dismay and, hearing the noise, Edwin Garland came from the living-room, where he had been having a Sunday afternoon snooze.

"What *is* this?"

"Pelagia won't be able to go on the tour!" Delphine announced. She had rather enjoyed the whole business, having a strong feeling for the dramatic, but she was naturally sorry about her sister's misfortune.

"Shut up, you little horror!" Anne said savagely. It was one more trouble on top of all the others and she was by now convinced that fate had turned unkind, not only to herself but to poor, inoffensive Pelagia.

"I'm not a horror! She won't, as anyone can see with half an eye. I'm terribly sorry, but what's the use –"

"Wait till the doctor comes," said her father and went to the telephone. While he was still there Mona Garland came downstairs and stared in dismay at the figures grouped round the sofa.

"Oh, Pel! What's happened?"

"Someone pushed me ... those awful stairs," said Pelagia.

"Oh, my dear, and the tour! We'd better get you a bandage –"

"Annali's gone for cold-water bandages," said Anne.

The doctor arrived within half an hour and was quite definite in his diagnosis.

"A very bad sprain indeed and a muscle pulled, too, at the back of the leg. She'll not dance for some time. Tour? A week on Friday? Not a hope. It'll be a month to five weeks before that leg's strong enough for ballet dancing. The sort of intensive dancing she'd have to do on tour, anyway. I'm very sorry, but there it is. She'd better stay in bed for two or three days to make certain of resting properly, and after that we'll see. Another few days on the sofa, at the very least."

Pelagia, forgetting that she was nearly eighteen, cried brokenly and refused to be comforted, and everyone in the house behaved so much as though a major tragedy had occurred that Joan was bewildered and, in her heart, coldly scornful. It *was* hard on Pelagia, of course. It was dreadful to miss dancing in Paris and Milan and all those other places, but, so fresh from real, irrevocable tragedy herself, she found the Garlands' extravagant dismay hard to bear.

All the same, it probably *was* her fault, and she went shyly and awkwardly into Pelagia's room later that evening.

"I'm so sorry. It was partly my fault –"

"*Your* fault? Of course not," said Pelagia thickly from the depths of her pillow. "I should have bought some other shoes, but I thought I'd get them in Paris. Oh, I shall never get over this. My first tour – Italy!"

Delphine arrived noisily.

"He telephoned – that nice young man. His name is Timothy Blandford. He asked me to tell you how sorry he is about missing the tour."

"Very nice of him," said Pelagia, without the faintest interest.

"He's great. He said that someone told him we were Mona Garland's children."

"Oh, go away!" Pelagia wailed. "Leave me to my sorrow! Did Mother telephone Mr Thorburg?"

"Yes," said Anne, appearing quietly. "He says he's more sorry than he can say. And if you should be better in time you can fly out to join them all later."

"I shall be dead of sheer heartbreak by then!" Pelagia said dramatically and burst into fresh floods of tears.

Chapter Eight

Before the Tour

In the general upset and dismay over Pelagia's accident, Joan was to a large extent overlooked for the next few days. She had already decided that it was easier to be ignored in the Garland household than drawn into their difficult conversations.

On Monday the younger ones poured off to school, Edwin and Mona Garland departed for a Company rehearsal and Pelagia was left to suffer, her sorrows perhaps a little mitigated – though, to judge by her crossness, one would never have known it – by constant offers of cold drinks, ice cream and other delicacies by the devoted Annali and Rosa.

Joan did the shopping and already she found that she was growing a little used to the Cockney voices. Annali, in her turn, had found that the Lancashire cousin was a good and careful shopper, insisting on getting value for money, unlike Anne and Delphine, who often brought home things that she certainly hadn't asked for and often at a higher price than Annali's thrifty Swiss soul could bear.

Returning with a laden basket and a scarlet string bag, Joan spied a faintly familiar figure walking slowly up and down the crescent. As she drew nearer she recognized the young man who had helped Pelagia in the Tower. He was carrying a vast bouquet of roses and carnations.

He grinned and saluted her. He was hatless and his hair looked bright in the sun.

"Thank goodness! I was just going to give up and go home. Not enough courage. You are one of them, aren't you?"

"I'm not a Garland. I'm their cousin, Joan Bradshaw."

"But you were at the Tower?"

"Fancy your noticing me!" said Joan, more with wonder than any intended sarcasm, but the young man flushed.

"I must admit I was mostly noticing Pelagia. Look here! Can't you give her these and say – ask her ... Couldn't I see her for a moment?"

"I don't know. She's still crying off and on. It was to have been her first tour."

"Oh dear! But I might cheer her up. Is she by herself?"

"Oh, yes. They've all gone off. School and rehearsals and classes. The whole set-up."

He looked surprised at her blunt and uncompromising tone.

"The little one said on the telephone that they were all dancers. Mona Garland! Fancy! I often used to wait at the stage-door to see her. But Pelagia ... Aren't *you* a dancer?"

"Do I look like one? No, I'm from Rochdale. I don't belong. I'll ask Pelagia. Just ... You'd better wait in here." And she showed him into the living-room and went upstairs with the flowers in her arms.

Pelagia looked up, startled. Her eyes were red, but she had tied back her hair with an emerald green ribbon and had a paler green shawl round her shoulders.

"That young man? What did Delph say he was called? Timothy Something? But why isn't he at work on a Monday morning? Oh, yes, send him up. I could do with an admirer. Not that I really care about *anything*, but they are gorgeous flowers. Tell him only for five minutes."

Joan looked into the living-room and found Timothy Blandford anxiously facing the door.

"She says will you come up, but only for five minutes."

In Joan's view it wasn't quite suitable for Pelagia to receive a strange young man in her bedroom, but no doubt the Garlands would think it all right.

Timothy followed her eagerly.

"Such luck I'm on holiday until Wednesday! I work for my father. He's an exporter in the City. I've been to France, but I got back –"

"Better not tell Pelagia."

"Oh, rather not," he agreed quickly. "She must be sick with disappointment. I say! It was kind of you!"

"Always ready to oblige," said Joan, a little amused. He looked nice, and he was so obviously attracted to Pelagia.

The small incident cheered her oddly for the rest of the morning, but there was not much else to cheer or amuse her. She was deeply uneasy about the new school and dreading the next morning.

That evening all the talk was about Pelagia, with some curiosity over Timothy Blandford, and the happenings of the day. No one even seemed to have remembered about the Scott-Smithson until Joan was on her way to bed and then her aunt followed her up the stairs.

"Is your uniform quite ready, dear? I do hope you like the school. And remember, you're to invite anyone you like here. To lunch or tea or anything you think best. It's your home, Joan. Do as you like."

Joan merely looked at her, and she went on: "You don't believe me? Oh, dear! You must think us utterly self-centred, but things are worse just now with the tour coming off and so much to arrange. And I don't know what's come over Anne. She's so quiet and worried-looking. Something to do with Lisa, and I don't think she likes having that Helenka Koronov back at the Thorburg.

You'll really have to accept us as we are. We mean well. We want you to feel at home."

"Yes, I know. Thank you," was all that Joan could manage to say, and Mona Garland sighed and went away slowly, after kissing her goodnight ...

Joan herself, conscious of ungraciousness and half-hating her aunt, undressed and bathed and then stood by her window in her pyjamas, seeing, not the narrow gardens and tall roof-tops of London, but that other view that she had taken so much for granted from her window at home. Home.

"Oh, Mother! Mother!"

And she flung herself into bed and sobbed into the sheet.

The next morning, however, she was pale and composed, wearing her new uniform.

"It does suit you," said Anne, as she rose from the breakfast table. "Sorry we've got to fly. Lucky you to be so near your school! Good luck!"

Joan set off grimly, with her new and almost empty satchel slung carelessly over one shoulder. Mona Garland had wanted her to have one of the little cases favoured by her own daughters, but she had insisted that she preferred a satchel. Elegant little boxes with fancy linings and handles were all right for prospective ballet dancers, but *she* was a prospective school teacher and might as well remember it.

She walked more and more slowly as she neared Dorset Square, not in the least cheered to see girls of all ages converging in front of the Scott-Smithson School. There would not be nearly so many pupils, of course, as at her old school, but this was an alien breed – Londoners, sophisticated, probably quite rich. Yes, there was a huge, shining car just stopping. A chauffeur!

Joan's pride forced her on and she reached the steps looking aggressive rather than shy. A few of the chattering girls gave her doubtful smiles, but she didn't smile back. They'd soon find out that she wasn't one of them, just as she wasn't one of the Garlands. She considered herself clever enough to get by at lessons in any school, but it wasn't that. It was just ordinary conversation. No doubt all these girls were familiar with the theatre, and went riding and for wonderful holidays abroad. They would hold some of the same odd views as the Garlands and discuss quite casually any number of things that would have been considered unsuitable, even "not quite nice", in a Lancashire village.

She went into the entrance hall in the midst of the crowd, but was almost at once singled out by a young and pretty teacher, who smiled and asked: "New, aren't you, dear? Joan Bradshaw? Yes." And Joan's name was ticked off on a list. "Look! I'll show you your cloakroom and perhaps we can find ... Oh, yes, Margaret MacAllister, who is new, too. Margaret, this is Joan Bradshaw, who'll be in your form. Just change your shoes and someone will show you both the way to the hall. We always have Assembly before classes."

Joan's aggression quickly died as she looked at the girl called Margaret. She had brown hair and she looked very definitely shy *and* scared. When she spoke her voice had a soft and appealing lilt that Joan had never heard before. Rather like Welsh, but very much softer.

"I'm so glad ... All the others seem to know each other. I felt – I very nearly ran away again." She said "fery."

"So did I," Joan confessed. "Are you – you don't sound like a Londoner."

"Neither do you," said Margaret, with a small smile.

"I'm not. I'm from near Rochdale in Lancashire. I've come to live with some cousins near here. In Moone Crescent."

"Oh, that's near Sussex Mews, isn't it? That's where I

live. We've been here for three weeks. I come from the Outer Isles and really I like to be called Peigi."

"That's Scotland, isn't it? The Outer Hebrides?"

"Yes. We lived on the Island of South Uist. Father's a writer. We lived in Edinburgh when I was little and then we went to Uist when I was five. I nearly died when Father made up his mind to come and live in London, but they said – said it would be best for me. I've never been to school – I had to have a governess, it was so remote – and I – I hadn't even seen a train since I was little ..."

A bell shrilled and someone said: "Come on, you two! This way. We'll show you."

Joan and Margaret followed obediently, eyeing each other with shy but growing awareness.

Joan said, as they went into the hall, which was built on at the back: "I *have* been to school. A big one. I suppose it isn't so bad for me."

"Oh, you can tell me things. I'm so very much afraid of making a fool of myself. You *will*, won't you?"

"I'll try, of course, but this is going to be very different from my old school."

"But you can cope with anything. You look so confident."

"If you only knew!" said Joan, with a flash of amusement, but the first nightmare feeling of strangeness had faded. It was a curious coincidence that she and the girl from South Uist had come together at once ... two strangers in – well, it was really a strange land for both of them. London after a remote island and after the northern moors! By the time they had managed to find an empty desk each, she was feeling a good deal more resigned to the Scott-Smithson School, though the feeling nearly didn't survive the mid-morning break, when her worst fears were realized. Everyone was talking about holidays abroad and about plans for the winter. Riding ... theatres ... clubs ... dancing classes.

Of course, if she said loudly and clearly that Mona

Garland was her aunt, that would almost certainly impress people. She might find herself in demand just because they would like to be asked to the house in Moone Crescent, on the chance of meeting the famous ballerina. But that she would not do. When Margaret found out she would be sworn to secrecy.

Joan was determined to make her own way, without leaning on the prestige of the name of Garland.

Meanwhile, at the Thorburg School, Anne was finding life anything but easy. At times, of course, she was happy. She always enjoyed the ballet classes that started each day, and usually she enjoyed her school work. But Lisa continued to be in mysteriously low spirits, refusing point blank to discuss her troubles, and there was also the problem of Helenka.

After that first moment of coming face to face, Helenka had ignored Anne, and Anne told herself that she was relieved. All the same, it was very uncomfortable. It was more uncomfortable still when they were bracketted with top marks for a special essay, and she knew that many of the others were looking curiously at them, remembering that old troublesome rivalry. Helenka herself looked straight ahead with a remote and vaguely scornful expression.

"I won't let it start again. I won't!" Anne thought. 'I'll let her win and she looks as though she means to. She's quieter, and different in some ways, but people don't change all that much."

"Aren't you going to let bygones be bygones?" Marris Mayhew asked, during break. Her tone was rather accusing and Anne flushed. Marris had been there during that awful Christmas term and had been one of the few who admired and was friendly with Helenka.

"What do you mean?"

"Cutting Helenka on the first day. She told me. She remembered you and was going to speak –"

"I should hardly think she could have forgotten me," said Anne.

"Well, it was six of one and half-a-dozen of the other, wasn't it?" Marris said. "And she's had a lot of trouble. Her father's dead, you know, and she and her mother ..."

"I didn't know about her father. I'm sorry," said Anne, with a surge of guilt. "But she'll make other friends. She doesn't want me. It didn't work before – our relationship, and – Oh, mind your own business, Marris! You always were a frightful busybody!"

"Oh, of course, Anne. I forgot you were a Garland. You all think you can go your own way ..."

"We don't," said poor Anne. "I didn't mean that. But, really, you must mind your own business about Helenka and me. I don't want any more trouble. All I want is a peaceful life."

"Take no notice of her," said Colin, who had overheard some of this conversation. "Some people can't keep their fingers out of pies. Just do as you think best."

"But is it best? I can't quite make Helenka out. Only she looks so superior. Sort of coldly proud, like a Russian princess. I never knew, until lately, just how hard people can be to understand."

"Oh, take them at their face value. It's easier."

It might be, but Anne could never quite forget Helenka's presence. Wherever she looked she seemed to see that rather cold profile that might mask anything. Was Helenka miserable, perhaps? Or just still convinced of her own superiority? It was impossible to tell.

Anne, in any case, had yet another problem, and that was Delphine's decidedly difficult behaviour during the first days of term. She was constantly in trouble and Anne heard endless tales. Delphine showed off in the ballet class and took criticism very badly; was naughty during ordinary lessons, and several times, in her general behaviour about the building, brought herself to the notice of the senior students and once came up against the headmistress herself. She did not respect people and seemed only bent on establishing the fact that Delphine Garland wouldn't be "downed" by anyone.

"They didn't want me," was all she would say in answer to the remonstrances of her elders. "And I don't particularly want to stay. I can't see why I shouldn't have been watching that senior class. They'd never even have known I was there if that bit of plywood hadn't fallen. I was behind it, with a lovely peep-hole. I don't see why they didn't think it good that I wanted to see the older ones."

"Because you should have been somewhere else, of course. And then there was that business of parading in Miss Grant's hat and coat."

"Oh, that was nothing. I was only amusing a few of our class. She was late. She left her things on a chair in the passage."

"You go on like the Naughtiest Girl in the School," said Anne, who had once had a brief passion for school stories.

"And shaming us all," added Edward.

Mona Garland heard about her youngest daughter's unsatisfactory behaviour and, whilst rushing around, found time to give her a long and stern lecture.

"I never thought that a child of mine would behave so stupidly," she ended. "Now I mean it, Delph. You've got to pull your socks up while we're away. If we come back and hear –"

"I hope you'll come back and hear that I'm in the Christmas Show."

"Not a hope of it, if you don't behave. And even if you do you know that only a very few are chosen out of each class."

"But it would be a mortal insult not to be chosen."

"Rubbish! All you've got to do is to settle down to your

school work and dancing and make reasonably good progress. No one will ask more of you for quite a few years to come."

"But that's dull! Some girls of my age have acted in films or won cups ..."

"We've never gone cup-hunting, as you know very well, and it would be frowned on at Thorburg. Now be sensible, Delph dear. We want to be proud of you."

And Delphine, suddenly altogether appealing, flung herself into her mother's arms and promised to be better. But the next day she was in trouble again for being rude to one of the most illustrious Seniors, a promising dancer who would soon be transferred to the Company.

"I never said anything!" Delphine complained later, in pained tones. "Only that she needn't think herself royalty just because of her age. I shan't be ten forever. It's just a misfortune that I suffer from at the moment. One day I shall be the second Fonteyn and no thanks to the Thorburg, either."

Her horrified family threw up their hands and looked at her in despair. Without doubt Delphine was thoroughly above herself and only a real shock could bring her to her senses.

So the days passed, with Joan finding school much more bearable than she had expected, but at home she was still very silent and had really made no progress at all with her cousins. In fact she saw little of them, except at meals, and, though they often tried to draw her into the conversation, she made it extremely difficult for them. She knew this and wished she could be more friendly to them, but somehow she didn't know how to start.

Pelagia, by now downstairs on the sofa, continued to behave like a tragedy queen, vowing that she would go into a decline as she lay there thinking of the Company flying away to Paris. She was limping about by the time the departure of the Company drew near, but was not even consoled by the fact that Timothy Blandford was a frequent caller, always bringing flowers and magazines.

Her family were much intrigued by the infatuated young man. He was by no means the first, but Pelagia had never been so much in one place before and that gave Timothy a chance that his earlier rivals had not had.

"He's nice," she said loftily. "And jolly intelligent. But of course it isn't serious. I haven't normally time for love. He understands that dancing is my life. I shan't marry until I'm at least thirty."

"I did," said Mona Garland.

"You must have been swept off your feet," Pelagia said, smiling at her mother. "I haven't been, and I don't mean to be. When I do marry it will have to be to someone who is a dancer. It's the only way to make it work."

"Well, let's hope that he really understands. He's not a boy. He must be at least twenty-two."

"As far as modesty permits," said Pelagia demurely, "I've made it plain. But he doesn't seem to believe me. I can't help that, can I? Oh, to think that this time next week you'll be dancing in Paris: walking along the boulevards, seeing those gorgeous shops! And Switzerland and Italy ... Oh, I'm the most unfortunate girl in the world."

It was the way most conversations ended and Joan could have slapped her. But, all the same, there were times when she found her eldest cousin both appealing and amusing. Perhaps more than any of them Pelagia belonged to an alien but intriguing world.

Chapter Nine

"I Don't Want to be a Dancer!"

The hall was filled with luggage and the whole house was in a turmoil on the day that the Thorburg Company was to leave for Paris. It was a Friday so the younger ones had to go to school as usual.

"You'll be there this afternoon and rehearsing tomorrow and Sunday," Anne said enviously, as she kissed her mother goodbye. "We shall follow you every step of the way in imagination. Oh, I hope it's the greatest success and that the critics are kind."

"Johann telephoned Paris last night," said her mother. "The theatre's fully booked for every performance."

"That's as it should be," said Anne with satisfaction.

"And you're all to be good and sensible and give Annali no trouble. Remember what I said to you last night, won't you, Bunch?"

Anne nodded, rather gloomily. They had had a private talk at bedtime, mainly about Joan. Her mother had said that she hoped, by the time they came back, that Joan would be much happier and far more a part of the household.

"She's so quiet and withdrawn," she had said, looking worried. "Though she does seem to like school and that quiet little Scottish girl she brought home once. Peggy, was it? But I want her to feel one of us."

"Oh, Mother. I'm sure she doesn't like us. And there's so little time."

"Well, do try. You're warm-hearted and I'm sure you can make friends. Just do your best, as you always do."

So that Friday morning Edward, Anne and Delphine said their goodbyes and dashed away, and Joan, leaving last as usual, found herself warmly kissed by her sweet-smelling aunt. As usual she held herself rigidly, though in her heart she liked being kissed. But it always embarrassed her a little; she and her mother had only very rarely been demonstrative.

"Goodbye, dear. We'll send you lots of postcards and we'll telephone."

"Telephone?" The thought of anyone having the money to telephone all the way from Switzerland or Italy astonished Joan.

"Of course. We always do. Work hard at school and try to be happy."

"I think I'll be top in English this week, and perhaps in history, too."

"That's splendid! A pity you can't influence Delph! Goodbye, then."

And Joan hurried away to meet Margaret on the corner of the crescent.

Their friendship was proving valuable to both of them, and they had found that they had much in common. In the first place there had been their shared strangeness in London and their homesickness for the lonely places they had known, but it hadn't stopped there. They liked the same books and periods of history, the same poetry, and in many ways shared the same ideas, though their upbringings had been so different. In fact there was that nameless sympathy and understanding between them that made for real friendship.

Joan was fascinated to hear about the lovely, remote island, with its great white western beaches, its solitary croft-houses, and its way of life that had, until recently, changed little for centuries. Then a missile range was built and this changed things and it was partly this that had decided the MacAllisters to move.

"Some of the people didn't mind," Margaret said once, as they strolled through the streets of Marylebone. "All the new people brought trade and better roads – that kind of thing. But it was sort of frightening, and Father hated the very thought of it. He gets really worked up on the subject of nuclear bombs and power, and modern warfare generally. Besides, he grew up in London and he wanted me to know it. But I was so scared of it at first, and I was so very homesick – not hearing the Gaelic, not feeling a real wind, or smelling the sea."

Joan, in her turn, told a good deal about her previous life, and dwelt briefly on her mother's sudden death and her arrival in the Garland household. Margaret, knowing, if anything, less about ballet than Joan herself, fully sympathized with the strangeness of it and readily promised to keep the secret from the other girls at school.

"They'll find out, I suppose," said Joan. "But I don't mean to tell them."

Together, after school, they began to explore the district, and found it one of great contrasts. As well as the park and the huge, elegant terraces and the quiet, charmingly painted mews houses, there were shabby narrow streets, the echoing coldness of Marylebone Station, and the Marylebone Road, with the Town Hall, the "skyscraper" and shops. They planned to wander farther afield and even to go to the Tate Gallery on Saturday afternoon.

"Because the others don't really want to bother with me," said Joan. "They're too completely absorbed in that ballet world of theirs."

Anne, at least, was completely absorbed, though not very happily. Never, since that long ago term of trouble, had she been so unhappy at her beloved Thorburg School. If only Lisa would confide in her; that would make things a little less bad and frightening. For she was convinced by now that Lisa was in some real and insoluble trouble, but was at a loss to guess what it could be.

That Friday when the Thorburg Company left for the Continent she said to Lisa after school: "Don't let's go home. Let's ring up and say we're having some tea out. I've got some money."

And, Lisa agreeing, they slipped away together and went to a coffee bar in Southampton Row. They were both rather silent over tea, when they had exhausted the subject of the tour, but both knew that they didn't want to separate.

After tea they went by bus to the south end of Regent's Park and walked slowly up the whole length of the Broad Walk. Autumn was coming rapidly now and the trees were beginning to show splashes of red and gold here and there, though there was still plenty of green. There were michaelmas daisies and brilliant dahlias in the beds, and a faint, lingering scent of bonfires.

"It's kind of sad," said Anne, sniffing the fragrant air. "But I love London at any time of the year."

They circled the Zoo, crossed the road and began to climb up Primrose Hill. The air was turning softly blue as the sun sank and the smell of bonfires was much stronger. Smoke drifted through the trees ahead of them.

They climbed to the highest point and turned to see the familiar sight of the city spread out below them.

It was warm and still and there were not many people around. Anne flung herself on the grass and put out her hand to pull Lisa down beside her.

"Tell me, then. You do mean to, only you've been putting it off for hours. I can't bear it much longer. I did think we were friends. You feel more like a sister than Pelagia or Delph sometimes."

Lisa dropped down and buried her face in the short grass. When she spoke her voice was shaky.

"I'm sorry, Bunch. I truly am. But I've been trying to get it straight; trying to see if it would go away and leave me as I was before. I knew you'd be so shocked and horrified. Almost as horrified as Father will be when I tell him. It'll break his heart. When it happened over Jocheli –"

Anne knew then. She wondered how she could have been so stupid as not to guess long before.

"Oh, Lisa, it's dancing! You don't care any more. You want to give it up."

Lisa began to cry into the grass, her thin shoulders shaking.

"I'm sorry! I'm a f-fool! But I've bottled it up for so long. I don't want to be a dancer. I thought I did at first. One has to start so young. But I've seen more and more clearly that I don't want it. I don't want to spend my life at the Thorburg and then in the Company. I want to do other things. I want to meet different people; people who have never heard of ballet. I want to do something real."

Anne gasped out of her deep bewilderment and dismay: "But it is real, isn't it? Ballet. To me it's the most real thing in the world."

"To you, yes. To all of you Garlands, except perhaps to Delphine. She isn't the dedicated type, though she may work hard in the end. But she'll probably prefer something livelier than ballet: musical comedy or something. Like you I've grown up with ballet – talked about it at every meal, watched it since I was in my cradle. When Jocheli said that he didn't want to dance – and that was when he'd been at the Thorburg for a year – I was shocked to the core, along with Father. Even Mother was shocked; she had taken it for granted that there were two prospective dancers in the family. And now there isn't *one*."

"But, Lisa, it will break your father's heart. Can you do that?"

Lisa's shoulders continued to shake.

"That's why I've been feeling so terribly bad. But it wouldn't be right to go on. I'm taking a place at the Thorburg that someone who really cares ought to fill. And in the end – it's started already – people would know my heart wasn't in it. And that would mean I wasn't good enough. Even if I put if off, Father would get to know, so I shall have to tell him, and I'm going to do it tonight."

"But, Lisa, I can't bear it, either. The Thorburg without you –"

"I know. I'm sorry. But we'll still be friends –"

"Not in the same way," said Anne, with dreary certainty. "Because I do feel that ballet is the only thing. I am dedicated. We'd soon grow far apart."

"We needn't. Not if you really feel as though I'm a sister. It might even make us better and more interesting friends."

"I don't really believe it. And – what is it that you want to do?"

"I want to go to an ordinary school after Christmas. I want to be able to ride and skate and do all sorts of other things without having to bother so much about sprained ankles and other injuries. I want to meet people with all sorts of interests, and I think that some day I'd like to specialize in languages. Go to a university and then get a job that is something to do with travelling. Be a courier … or a hostess at a holiday place on the Continent … Something that would take me about."

"But – but you'd travel a lot as a dancer."

"Yes, but I don't want to spend my whole life grinding away at the *barre*. You see, I have found it a grind lately."

"Drudgery," Anne said slowly.

"Yes. Just that."

"Joan called it drudgery, but Joan doesn't understand anything. Or I thought she didn't. I never thought that you – you –" And Anne stared at the darkening view, in which lights were beginning to shine, with blurred eyes.

Lisa sat up. She was very white, but composed now.

"Bunch, tell me honestly? Do you really, in your heart of hearts, think I've got the makings of a ballerina?"

"How can I say? How can anyone say? You're not quite fourteen. It's too young; too early." But Anne's gaze was the one that fell.

"You see, you don't think so. I haven't got the spark. One can't really tell, but I know it, all the same. Don't forget that for all the hundreds and thousands who learn to dance there can only be a few ballerinas. I am Johann Thorburg's daughter and I ought to know that better than most people. There are plenty who, though they give their hearts and bodies to ballet for many years, never get beyond being reliable soloists. There are countless more who stay in the *corps*, or never even get that far. I would almost certainly get into the Company if I stayed and worked, but I'm not prepared to give up my whole life and only stick in the *corps* in the end. *You* would be."

Anne shivered, though it was not cold.

"Yes, I would be. I have to have ballet on any terms. To be shut out of the theatre would be like being shut out of heaven."

Lisa laughed.

"I suspect that that's a sort of blasphemy."

"You know what I mean. I'd sooner be dead. And so would Pelagia and so would Edward."

"But not Delphine?"

"Oh, who knows what that little idiot really feels? She may turn out to be the one – the great one. Though I agree with you that it's almost too much to hope that a family will turn out a great one at all."

"Well, your mother is Mona Garland. What's bred in the bone ..."

"And your father is Johann Thorburg." For Johann Thorburg had once been a dancer of note, before he gave up his time to administration and choreography.

"Yes," Lisa agreed soberly. "The argument doesn't work. I'm truly sorry, Bunch, but I mean it. I'm going home now to talk to Father. He isn't going to the theatre tonight. He's waiting at home for a call from America or somewhere. He told me this morning."

"I shall never be able to bear it. I shall pray that you change your mind."

"Don't, because I shan't."

They parted sadly at the foot of the hill and Anne turned to walk round the outside of Regent's Park. It was nearly dark, but a great full moon was coming up, glowing orange in the faint mist.

When she arrived home her brother, sisters and Joan were gathered in the living-room, Joan was absorbed in *Wuthering Heights*, but the others sat around looking glum. It was Friday, so homework could wait.

"I hate it when Father and Mother have just gone away," Delphine was saying drearily, and Pelagia began to wail: "In Paris! Think of it! Perhaps having dinner under the moon. It's quite warm enough. Oh, unkind fate –"

"What's the matter, Bunch?" Edward asked, seeing Anne's face as she stood in the doorway. Her jacket was unbuttoned and her Thorburg beret pushed rakishly back on her untidy hair.

"Something awful!" said Anne, putting down her case and flinging herself into a chair. "It isn't a secret. Not really, but don't talk about it to anyone at the Thorburg yet. Though I suppose they'll soon know." And she poured out a good deal of what Lisa had told her.

The news was received by everyone in the Garland

family with blank astonishment and dismay, and Joan put down her book and stared from one to the other.

"She must be mad!" exclaimed Pelagia, dragged out of her own disappointment by so startling a revelation. "Johann Thorburg's daughter! Why, he'll – he'll hit the roof. He's so proud of her. She had every chance of getting into the Company, and –"

"I suppose she's thought it out," said Edward at last.

"I think she's thought till she's sick. She doesn't seem mad; particularly sane, in fact, in most ways. Oh, I did all I could. She knows how much I'll mind," said Anne.

"I thought she was sure to turn into a ballerina," said Delphine, still wide-eyed.

"Oh, she wasn't. You ought to know that no one is. But she has years yet, and – Oh, isn't life terrible?" And Anne stared tragically into the small bright fire that Annali had lit to cheer those left unadventurously at home.

A few seconds later her eyes met Joan's and she said bitterly: "Well, go on, Joan. Tell us what *you* think. A fuss about nothing, I suppose?"

"Shhh!" said Pelagia.

"Why? We may as well know."

Joan had flushed deeply. She had been sitting there, feeling the complete outsider, as usual: the audience. If it hadn't been for Margaret, whom she now always thought of as Peigi, she sometimes thought she would never have borne it.

"Well, since you ask me," she said slowly, "I feel sorry for poor Lisa. If she wants to give up dancing she ought to be able to do it without having to feel guilty."

"Guilty! But ..."

"She's your friend. Oh, I don't mean to sound priggish, but oughtn't you to help her, not make things harder? She's got to face her father, and you as well. It seems to me rotten hard luck to have to comfort *two* people, when she probably needs comforting herself. Besides, it isn't a sin, or the end of the world, if someone doesn't want to dance."

Anne had sprung up half-way through Joan's speech, disregarding Pelagia's restraining hand.

"How can you? You don't understand anything! I do want to help her. And I didn't – didn't ask for your advice." She was on the verge of tears.

"Don't be a fool, Bunch," Edward said quietly, heartily wishing that he had removed himself from female company and gone to the cinema with Jocheli.

"You asked me what I thought," Joan said unhappily. "But I wish I hadn't answered. You are terribly lost in your ballet world, but there really are heaps of other things."

"I'm not lost! I've tried to think – to understand. You don't care twopence for ballet."

"No, you're wrong. I could care. But if Lisa had lost a leg or something while she still wanted to dance that would have been a tragedy. As it is she's simply made up her mind ..."

"Oh!" And Anne made for the door. They heard her pounding up the stairs and then her bedroom door slammed. There was an uncomfortable silence.

"She's thoroughly worked up lately," said Pelagia and reached out for the case of records at her side. "Let's have some music. Something loud and exciting."

"Arnold," suggested Edward. "That Scottish thing when the strings are bagpipes. *Tam O'Shanter*. And isn't it bedtime for you, Delph?"

"I guess so," agreed Delphine, with unusual willingness. There was an American child in her class and she had been adopting new expressions and turns of speech lately.

"Buzz off, then."

After a few moments Joan followed her. Once more she had said the wrong thing, though pity for Lisa had been the driving force. She hesitated on the landing, fighting pride and shyness, and eventually knocked gently and opened the door of the room shared by Anne and Pelagia.

Anne was fiercely brushing her hair, her shoulders shaking a little.

"Anne, I – I'm sorry. I didn't mean to upset you more. Perhaps I don't understand."

"It's OK. Forget it. It's just life's so – so difficult."

"It is for me, too," Joan said, before she could stop herself and for a moment they stared at each other.

"I know," said Anne, with compunction. "I have meant to help more, only – only ... Oh, please do leave me alone now."

Joan crept away and Anne continued to brush her hair. She was admitting to herself that Joan's words had been true.

"Oughtn't you to be helping her?" "Why should she have to feel guilty?" "You're lost in your ballet world."

Though it was quite a long time before Anne realized it consciously, her new awareness dated from that unhappy evening. After that she never quite took things for granted again and she found it easier to look out of "the ballet world".

Chapter Ten

Joan and Ballet

The next afternoon Anne, Colin and Lisa were going to Covent Garden to see *Sylvia* in their usual seats at the front of the amphitheatre. This had been arranged quite a long time before and ordinarily Anne would have been looking forward to it, for, though she often played the record, she had only seen *Sylvia* once.

But she awoke with a headache, and a heartache as well, and breakfast was a rather uncomfortable meal, in some ways, with Edward absorbed in his letters – he was a great letter-writer and received a good many in return – and Pelagia glum, since she was remembering that, that very morning, rehearsals would be starting in the Paris theatre.

Anne drank some orange juice, followed it with a piece of toast and a cup of milky coffee, and then stole away to the telephone in her father's study.

"Lisa!" she cried, when she heard her friend's voice. "Oh, Lisa, how did it go? What did your father say?"

Lisa, surprisingly, sounded a good deal more cheerful than she had done the previous evening.

"Oh, Bunch, he was splendid. He was so kind and understanding, and he said he'd been expecting something of the kind. He does mind – I know he does, because now he can't pass on the Thorburg to either of us, as I believe he always hoped – but he told me not to worry and he only wanted me to be happy. We talked and talked, and Mother came in after a while, and I'm to finish at the Thorburg at Christmas and to go to another school in the New Year. I might go to the Scott-Smithson with your Joan. The older girls can specialize in languages there, and Father says that's a good idea. I can speak German already, as you know, and my French isn't bad. I shall probably learn Italian and Spanish as well, or even Russian. So I feel – oh, so much better! As though a weight has rolled off me. But I still mind dreadfully about you."

"You needn't," Anne said steadily. "I've thought it over and I see that I was very selfish. I shall miss you dreadfully – but of course we'll still be friends. Nothing could stop that."

"Oh, Bunch, I'm glad!"

"But, Lisa, about this afternoon. Do you still want to go to Covent Garden?"

"Yes," said Lisa. "I do now. I shall always love watching ballet and I won't give that up. I'll call for you after lunch."

So Anne, too, felt more cheerful, though her heart still sank when she thought of the Thorburg without Lisa. And when she, Lisa and Colin climbed the stairs to the amphitheatre a few hours later it seemed as though things had not really changed. They had been there so often, high, high above the big stage.

"I wish we could always afford to go in better seats, all the same," Anne confessed, as they looked down at the assembling people.

"Oh, I don't know. I like being in the amphitheatre," said Lisa, and they all studied their programmes until the houselights began to fade. Anne muttered to Lisa: "Shall you tell him?" And Lisa mumbled back: "After. We'll go and have tea and buns and tell him then. Everyone will have to know, but my friends must know first."

And then they were in that other world, watching the Nymphs and Sylvans dancing before the shrine of Eros, waiting for that wonderful, exciting moment when Sylvia came leaping on to the stage. Anne's scalp prickled at the sound of the hunting horns and the wild beating of the drums. Even just listening to the music on a record she was always conscious of the thrill of it. And here she was, Sylvia! Fair, beautiful and proud, watched secretly by Aminta, the shepherd lad.

"It was splendid!" said Colin, as they emerged, blinking, into the mellow late afternoon light. "It has some grand moments, in spite of the silly story. When Diana bursts out of the temple ..."

"I shall always like the drum part best," said Anne. "If I were dying and they played that I think I should come back to life. Did you – did you enjoy it, Lisa?"

All the time she had been conscious of her friend at her side, wondering how she was feeling now that she had given up forever all chance of dancing Sylvia, or any other role.

"Yes," said Lisa, gravely. "More than anything for a long time. I could give my mind to it."

"Why couldn't you before?" asked Colin curiously, and, as they walked down Wellington Street into the Strand, Lisa told him her news. He listened in wide-eyed dismay.

"But – but are you sure? We all thought – everyone thinks – you belong to the Thorburg."

"Not any more. Not after Christmas. Yes, I am sure. You can tell the others, Colin. It isn't a secret."

They continued to talk about it over tea and cakes.

Meanwhile, Joan and Margaret had made their way to Westminster, and, after a peep into the Abbey, set off to walk along Millbank to the Tate Gallery. They paused often, first to stare at the Houses of Parliament, then at

Lambeth Palace on the other side of Lambeth Bridge, and then just to lean on the wall above the river, watching the barges and other craft. In the autumn sunshine London looked at its best, and they were completely at ease in each other's company.

"I'm getting to love London," Joan confessed. "At first I was scared; it seemed so huge and noisy and crowded; dreadfully impersonal. But now ... of course I do miss Lancashire and the hills and the people I used to know. Sometimes I feel quite ill with longing for the smell of the hills and the sound of the sheep and curlews."

"Smells are the worst," Margaret said wistfully. "I miss the smell of the sea, and of peat-smoke, and of the sea-wrack on the shore after a gale or a high tide. Shall we ever go back, do you think?"

"I mean to. I'm going to ask if I can stay with Mrs Thwaite either in the Christmas holidays or at Easter. Of course the fare costs a lot, but the Garlands don't seem to fuss much about money. And yet I don't think they're so very rich. Ballet dancers, even ballerinas, don't seem to make a fortune. I've heard Aunt Mona say that that's why she appears on television as often as she can. She gets a lot extra for that."

"It isn't money so much," Margaret said slowly. "The Isles are so far away. I couldn't go alone. They're as far as – oh, as far as Switzerland, I should think. But Father did promise ..."

"Oh, of course you will go back. But it is still interesting discovering London."

The two exiles walked on along Millbank, Joan much the taller, and soon they approached the impressive front entrance of the Tate Gallery. They climbed the steps and entered shyly, for neither had ever been to such a place before. However, no one took any notice of them and they were soon utterly fascinated by the pictures. Joan found the

Lowry, *The Pond*, and stared at it for a long time, and after that they found and admired some pictures by John and Paul Nash. They spent most of the rest of the time looking at the French Impressionist and post-Impressionist paintings, finding, to their delight, that they both liked these too.

"I wish I could see more Utrillos," Joan said presently. "I do love that little Montmartre one – the little back street with just a touch of blue, and those lovely grey-white walls – and the *Place du Tertre*. Oh, and the Cézannes and Van Goghs. Do you think we shall ever travel ... go to France?"

"Heaps of the others at school have been," said Margaret.

"Yes, they take it for granted. But then they're not like us."

"No," said Margaret, rather sadly. "They take so many things for granted. Father says I'm not to worry. He says I'll become sophisticated soon enough."

"I doubt if I ever shall," said Joan. "I wish everyone wouldn't think of Lancashire as darkest England. It makes me so cross. But there's no doubt – and I see it now – that there are a lot of things I haven't done and don't know. The things that the Garlands talk about."

It was certainly true that they were different from most of the girls of their age at the Scott-Smithson, many of whom had had, in some ways, more experiences. Alone at the school each would have been utterly miserable, but together they presented a united front. No one except Margaret knew about the Garlands. Joan was gradually making headway in the school. She worked well and intelligently. Good work was respected at the Scott-Smithson, and she was especially praised for her essays and for her original, unusual work in the art classes.

So in school, and exploring London with Margaret, she was happy, but at home she still felt the odd one out. Anne knew it, and, especially after that brief flash of understanding on the evening that Lisa's news was broken, honestly meant to do something about it, but she was busy and not very happy and there had not been a chance.

Things were by no means ideal at the Thorburg. Lisa's decision to leave and go to an ordinary school had been a nine days' wonder with most people, but, as the term wore on, there were other things to think about.

Anne was often very miserable about Lisa's going, but honestly did her best to keep her feelings from her friend. Then there was Helenka, and Anne was very uncomfortable about the Russian girl.

It was so very awkward to be in the same class and ignore each other, and it occasioned a lot of talk and speculation. But the ignoring had happened at once and Anne knew no way to alter things, even if she had wanted to do so. Helenka had a few friends, who seemed to admire and like her, but mostly she went her quiet way, looking proud, remote and vaguely tragic.

Whenever they actually came face to face she looked at Anne gravely and without embarrassment. It was always Anne who was embarrassed. But Helenka made no attempt to speak, and did, in fact, seem to go out of her way to avoid the girl who had once been her rival.

It became apparent as the term progressed that, whether they wished it or not, they were still rivals. Anne was one of the leading lights of her class. Her dancing had been improving steadily and now she was one of the best for her age. She earned a good deal of praise in the ballet classes, and so, after a few weeks, did Helenka. She had been a precocious and talented ten-year-old and now she had settled down to being a dancer of no mean ability. She had an ideal face and body for a ballet dancer, as all the teachers at the Thorburg were quick to note, and technically she was remarkably mature. She had had good teachers in

America and had not wasted her time.

In ordinary lessons, too, after she had surmounted the difficulties of the different methods of tuition, she was making good progress; in fact, her marks mounted each week. One week Anne had the highest marks, the next Helenka. Then came the day when they tied for top of the class.

Their form mistress knew the tensions between the two. She remembered the old trouble and had been disappointed to see that neither had forgotten or apparently forgiven. But she never made any comment, hoping that things would right themselves in the end. Anne Garland had good sense as well as a warm heart, and Helenka, after the troubled, even tragic time she had had in America, could do with plenty of friends.

So she announced the marks quietly and without looking closely at either of them. But she was aware of the stir in the class and of the curious glances directed from Anne to Helenka.

Anne stared down at her book, the colour dying her face rather unbecomingly, but Helenka stared straight ahead, looking quite unmoved.

"You'll have to watch her," someone said to Anne, as they went down to the cloakroom. "Remember the Christmas Show. The dancers will be chosen early in November. Odd if Helenka gets a good part and you don't." There was a trace of malice in the tone, for, though Anne was popular on the whole, people could never quite forget that her mother was a famous ballerina. There were many jealousies at the Thorburg, and, rightly or wrongly, her famous mother was felt to give Anne an advantage.

"If she does she does," said Anne calmly, though her heart sank. "She's a good dancer. She deserves it."

Anne's third worry concerned Delphine, who continued to get into trouble one way and another. In fact she was a by-word in the School and something of a joke with those who were not just plain irritated and annoyed with her. Delphine had personality and soon collected a number of admiring, but slightly alarmed followers. Anne constantly expected real trouble and often wished that her parents were home to deal with their youngest child.

But Mr and Mrs Garland were far away and their only real connection with Moone Crescent was the occasional telephone call from Paris, Zurich or some other city. And Pelagia, who might have been expected to try and talk some sense into Delphine, was back at ballet classes and was hoping to fly out to join the Company for their last week in Monte Carlo.

But one thing Anne tried to do. She did give Joan the opportunity to see some more ballet. It happened that their next-door neighbours, the Jollys, again couldn't use their seats for Covent Garden one Saturday evening in October. Mr Jolly's work often took him away from home unexpectedly and his wife sometimes with him.

"Who'll go?" Delphine demanded fiercely, when they were in possession of the two tickets for the Stalls Circle.

"Joan," Anne said promptly. "It's the first chance she's had."

"Good idea!" said Edward, who was busy anyway. "But who with?"

Anne hesitated. She didn't want to go with Joan; not really.

"Would your Peigi go, Joan?"

Joan looked startled.

"I don't know. I could ask. But don't you want them? Stalls Circle? Those are expensive seats, aren't they?"

"Yes, but that's better for you. You'll get a splendid view and it's *The Sleeping Beauty*. It's wonderful at the Garden. They have all the machinery to make it really impressive, as well as a big company. Besides, it's –" And she mentioned the greatest dancer of the day.

Joan went to the telephone and spoke to Margaret, who went away to ask for permission. She came back after rather a long time.

"I can go. Father and Mother said no at first. They think we're too young to go to an evening performance by ourselves. They're going to take us in the car and then they'll ask what time it will be over and meet us."

"That's very nice of them," said Joan, disappointed, all the same, that they would not have the pleasure that she had heard Anne talk about – of arriving at Covent Garden Underground station with all the other eager ballet-goers, and walking down Floral Street.

"We'll pick you up, then."

Joan was ready when the big, shabby car that the MacAllisters had brought with them from South Uist pulled up at the door.

Her head was spinning with information, for Anne and Delphine had plied her with details about the ballet, and Anne had even played the music for the Prologue and First Act, saying occasionally such things as: "This is the part where Carabosse, the Wicked Fairy, comes in – all dark and wild. That's the Lilac Fairy's own tune. Isn't it lovely? Now this is everyone assembling for the sixteenth birthday. Now the Garland Dance – you'll like that. And the Rose Adagio. Oh, I envy you seeing that tonight! It's one of my favourite bits of ballet. You must see Mother dance it one day. Now the Aurora Variations ..." and so on, determined to see that her cousin was not unprepared, but not sure if it was doing any good or if the information were welcome.

"I like the last act best," Delphine had chipped in. "The White Cat – I love that! And the Aurora *pas de deux* is perfect."

"My head is stuffed with Aurora Variations and *pas de deux*," Joan remarked, as she climbed into the back of the car with Margaret, having greeted Mr and Mrs MacAllister, whom she had met a number of times before. "And things about the scenery sticking. Once, when Anne was at Covent Garden, the fairy boat wouldn't move and the trees didn't grow round the Palace!"

"I should think it spoils it to think of things like that," said Mrs MacAllister.

"They don't think so," Joan said ruefully. "They know all the ins and outs, of course, and just how everything works, but they still seem to be able to lose themselves in it."

Eventually they nosed their way slowly round the corner towards the front of the Opera House, where taxis were drawing up and departing all the time.

Margaret gasped at the sight of the great pillared frontage, for, like Joan, she had scarcely ever been to a theatre.

"Sure you've got the tickets? And money for programmes? Then we'll be somewhere about here when you come out. We may have to drive round and round the block. Just stand out in front where we can see you."

Then Joan and Margaret were swept into the throng in the entrance hall and Joan found, a little to her amusement, that here she was supposed to take the lead. They walked slowly up the stairs into the theatre, awed and almost completely silenced by its lights and its red and gold splendour.

"Oh!" cried Margaret, when they were in their seats, which were splendid ones in the front row. "I feel like Cinderella at the Ball. What a wonderful, unbelievable place!" And she stared round with wide, astonished eyes, her gaze travelling from the Stalls below to the tiers and tiers of seats – Stalls Circle, Grand Tier, Balcony Stalls and Amphitheatre.

It was certainly different from the Thorburg and Joan was conscious of little prickles of delight and excitement.

"I am here at Covent Garden," she told herself, almost unbelieving. "Here in London at the Opera House. Oh,

Mother! Mother! What would you think if you could see me?"

But thoughts of her mother were beginning to hurt her less, and soon she was absorbed in her programme. Innumerable meals given over largely to ballet talk had familiarized her more than she had realized with the names, at least, of many dancers, and she was even able to supply some information.

"He's married to the girl who is dancing the Lilac Fairy. She's just been on tour with her partner to some of the northern cities. The conductor tonight used to be with the Liverpool Philharmonic."

"You do know a lot," said Margaret admiringly, rather bewildered by the very long cast.

"I can't help but pick up things. It's all part of the Garlands' world."

But she was startled by the strange surge of wistfulness and awareness that shot through her as the houselights slowly faded and the music started. Their world! Their fascinating, though at first half-despised world. And she was on the outside, never likely to belong. But why not try to belong? With a ballerina for an aunt and four dancing cousins, as well as an uncle who was a conductor, there ought to be some way in. Anne and Edward were often behind the scenes at the Thorburg; they had watched Company rehearsals, stood in the wings during the actual performance. They would be only too delighted, probably, to include her.

Then she remembered that she had deliberately held herself aloof, and there seemed no way, now, of breaking the invisible barrier.

The great red and gold curtain rose softly on the christening scene, and from the first moment Joan sat tense and completely absorbed, lost in the dancing of each fairy, thrilled by the moment when the stage darkened, the music grew loud and ominous, and Carabosse entered with her horrid attendants. But Carabosse did not have the last word – or, rather the last music. All, in the end, was well, in the best tradition of the fairy story. The Lilac Fairy's lovely music swelled out and the Princess would not die, but would sleep, when the time came, for a hundred years.

The way that the curtain came down in one heart-stopping sweep made her gasp.

"I never knew … I never imagined …!" Margaret cried, in her soft, lilting voice. "Oh, Joan, is this it? The thing all your relations do? Oh, Joan, you are lucky!"

"I didn't think so at first," Joan said slowly. "Oh, Peigi, the way that curtain came down! The cool, woody smell from the stage; did you notice it? The whole thing … It's a – a revelation!"

Still dazed, they followed the crowd and found themselves at the head of a great ornate staircase, with a huge chandelier above them, and then they were in the vast Crush Bar, with another chandelier and flowers and mirrors, feeling small and unimportant. They withdrew against a pillar and stared about them.

"But the ballerina?" Margaret said presently, as the crowd surged about them. "We haven't seen her yet."

"In the next act. The first act, they call it," said Joan. "Though it's really the second. The Christening is called the Prologue. She comes in after the Garland Dance and then it's the Rose Adagio with the four Princes. Anne played me the music."

And the Rose Adagio, when it came, was the most perfect thing that Joan had ever seen, danced by a famous ballerina who had perfected the role long ago, but who still brought something new and moving to each performance. Now, at last, Joan could see some sense and purpose in those endless hours at the *barre*. It was a striving for perfection. And the striving might bring, after many, many years, this lovely and perfect lyrical movement.

The Aurora Variations moved her nearly as much, and then came the tragedy of the pricked finger, the horror of the Court, and the Lilac Fairy's timely arrival to see that the Princess slept in the palace, surrounded by the growing trees. Softly, wherever the Lilac Fairy moved, the trees and bushes grew up, soft cobwebby gauzes came down, and the palace sank into its secluded hundred years of sleep.

The curtain swished down for a second time and there were two, at least, in the audience who could not bring themselves sufficiently into the real world to buy coffee or ice-cream.

"I see now what Delphine meant about the chocolates," Joan said. "I don't want them, do you?" For she had long ago told Margaret all about the first visit to the Thorburg Theatre.

"I don't want anything," said Margaret vaguely. "Only for it to go on. Why do they have to have so many intervals?"

"Well, to change the scene, and for them to have a rest, I suppose. Next it's the Vision scene, when the Prince leaves the hunting-party and the Lilac Fairy shows him a vision of the Princess. And then the last one is the wedding, with what they call a *divertissement*. Anne said we were to notice the Blue Bird *pas de deux* especially."

There was no danger of their not watching, and at the end of the long ballet they wandered out dreamily into Bow Street, clutching each other's hands.

"I loved it all," said Margaret. "And all the curtains at the end and the cheering and the flowers. If Father and Mother weren't coming for us we could wait at the stage-door and see her near to."

"I suppose we could. I've heard about that. Here at Covent Garden the ballerina comes into the stage-door office and people queue and go in one by one, to have their programmes signed."

"Alone with her? Really?"

"Well, just for a few moments. Anne went once for fun. Her family seemed to think it very odd of her. Of course they can get autographs other ways, if they want them. Aunt Mona knows most of the great dancers. Anne says that lots of famous dancers have come to parties at Moone Crescent."

"They might come again and you'd be there."

"I should be peering down the stairs, then," Joan said. "I don't know what to say to Pelagia, never mind to famous people."

"But your aunt is famous."

"I know. I still can't get used to it. She's very nice. Look! Isn't that your car?" And they darted round a stationary taxi and dived into the back seat.

Chapter Eleven

Joan and Music

Joan arrived home at Moone Crescent to find everyone except Pelagia – and Annali – in bed. Pelagia had been to the cinema with Timothy and was wolfing sandwiches and coffee in the hungry way that had surprised Joan so much at first. It still seemed astonishing to see an ethereal sylphide eating so much.

Pelagia looked in some surprise at her cousin whom she had always thought stodgy and unapproachable. Now Joan's soft dark hair was tumbled about a face that was unusually flushed, her eyes were bright and her expression alert.

"Sit down and have some," she invited, pushing forward the sandwiches. "The coffee's hot, but take plenty of milk or you'll never sleep. Did you enjoy it?"

"Oh, yes! It was wonderful! I – I thought that Covent Garden was splendid, and the dancing ..."

"The Garden's all right. A really thrilling place at its best. But you owe allegiance to the Thorburg, you know."

"Do I? I've only been there once."

"You do. We're all heart and soul with the Thorburg and you're part of the family, aren't you?"

"Not really," said Joan, eating a sandwich and finding

that she was ravenous. "I don't know the first thing."

"You can learn, can't you? Not to dance, of course, but all the rest. Then you'd have a foot in both worlds."

It was so much what Joan herself had been thinking that she was startled and suddenly shy.

"You – you don't want me, though. Why should you?"

Pelagia was a self-absorbed girl, without much imagination, but she was in a mellow mood. The film had been good, Timothy had paid her several heart-felt compliments – and it was always pleasant to be admired – and she was off to Monte Carlo at the end of the week.

"Well, I don't know. Why shouldn't we? We're a big enough family to take in another very happily. Only if you insist on being an outsider it's hard to do much. You and Anne should be friends."

"She's got Lisa, and Fernanda, and Colin Corbett and all the others."

"But you're here under the same roof, and the same age and everything."

"I can't – can't talk to Anne."

"Well, let her talk. She does plenty of it usually. You only need to sympathize and listen, and then gradually you'd talk and that would be that."

It sounded easy, but Joan was well aware that it would not be at all easy in practice.

"Anyway, I'd like to see more ballet."

"Good-o!" said Pelagia lazily. "Or fine, as Delph would say at the moment. What about the Ballet Rambert? They're on next week. A small company, but jolly good. We'll all go on Tuesday or Wednesday. I'll get seats for Tim and me and you and Anne. Ed goes his own way, mostly, but I suppose Delph will scream the place down if we leave her out, though she ought to go to bed early in term-time."

"Oh, you can't leave her out," Joan said laughing. She thought Delphine hopelessly spoilt, but it would be hard to have to stay at home while all the rest were enjoying themselves.

"Oh, all right. I'll see to it. Have the last sandwich; half were for you, anyway. Turn the light out, will you? I'm going up." And Pelagia went gracefully away, humming the Waltz of the Flowers from *Casse Noisette*.

So the following Wednesday evening Joan once more found herself in the theatre. Twice in less than a week! What would her mother have thought? The programme consisted of two short new ballets, with *Gala Performance* and *Les Sylphides*. It was all very different from Covent Garden, and not nearly so moving and exciting, but what she lost in emotional pleasure Joan gained in knowledge.

She had a good clear mind and, now that she had set herself to learn about ballet, concentrated on observing all she could, noticing the music, the sets, the costumes, and that still rather mysterious thing called the choreography – the dance movements. Already she was beginning to see the difference between classical and modern ballet and some of the meanings of the ballet terms were becoming clear. When Pelagia and Anne spoke about the male dancer's *grands jetés* she now knew that they were the great leaps that carried him across the stage. She knew what *pirouettes* were, and *fouettés*, and could recognize an *arabesque*. It was like learning a new language. She remembered the ideas she had once had for the scenery, costumes, story and music for a ballet, and thought that maybe one day she would make a real attempt to create something.

But she was so quiet that Anne and the others had no idea of all that was going on in her head. Anne asked at the end, politely: "Did you enjoy it, Joan?"

And Joan answered: "Yes, thank you. But not as much as *The Sleeping Beauty*."

"Oh, well, there's so much more to get *hold* of in the long ballets."

Pelagia left for the South of France, and things were, on the whole, very quiet for a week. In the evenings they all concentrated on homework, even Delphine who was bullied by Edward and Anne into doing some.

"Do you want them to think you stupid? Half-way down the class! It's a disgrace to the name of Garland. Get down to it, Delph."

And Delphine, grumbling fiercely, settled down to work.

The main source of excitement at the Thorburg was, of course, the coming Christmas Show, and even Edward seemed quite worked up about the chances of getting a good part.

"But you're sure to," said Anne. "I wish I'd been born a boy. It's far harder for girls. Too many of them."

The next day she came home in a flurry of excitement and despair.

"What do you think of the competition, Ed?" she asked, when her brother appeared shortly after her.

"Oh, nothing. I shan't go in for it. I'm a dancer, not an artist. They'll have to find new ballets without any help from me."

"I suppose I shan't, either. But I wish I could. I can see things in my own mind. I often think of ballets – book and costumes and décor and what music would be suitable – but I just can't draw and paint. Besides, there's so little time."

"Someone had a last-minute brainwave to see what we can do."

"What is it?" Joan asked curiously, and Anne looked at her in surprise, but answered readily: "It was up on the notice board. Anyone who likes can submit suggestions for a new short ballet, suitable for inclusion in the Christmas Show. That is, a suggested story, and costumes and a very simple set, and music, and suggestions for choreography. But the last isn't necessary. One of the ballet teachers, or perhaps Mr Thorburg himself, would do that. Oh, the Seniors will go in for it, choreography and all. It's right up their street. But I wish I could try."

"A ballet? A new ballet? A sylphide-y one?"

Anne laughed, struck by her cousin's interest.

"Any sort of ballet, I suppose. It needn't be classical. Better not, probably. Short, modern, simple. I wish I could do something to that *Tam O'Shanter* thing by Malcolm Arnold."

"Everyone in kilts," Edward suggested lightly.

"Oh, I don't know. I couldn't design a set and costumes to save my life, even though I know just what's wanted. I know just how simple it would have to be. They'll make the scenery in the Thorburg workshop and the costumes, too. But time will be short."

Joan finished the meal and then went slowly up to her room. She sat down on her bed and stared at the Lowry print. She had had vague ideas about creating a ballet for a long time and now she would try. Not sylphide-y ... something modern, like those two done by the Ballet Rambert. Not the Jacobite story she had once thought of, something else. Children in a Lancashire street ... mill chimneys and a row of houses with clean steps and brass knockers ... a procession, perhaps. What about that procession the Ukrainians used to put on a saint's day? *Street Scene ... The Day of the Procession ... The Procession Passes*. The last one was best.

She reached for a soft pencil and, on a large drawing-block that she had bought with some of her pocket-money, began to sketch. Simple ... Yes, of course. Just a backcloth, that was what they called it. And wings, those bits that jutted out sideways.

An hour later she sat staring at the drawing, which was

stark but telling. Colour, of course; there would have to be colour. The next step would be to paint it properly, and then perhaps to make a proper little stage, gumming the wings and curtain into place, like those models she had once seen in an exhibition.

Joan frowned and chewed her pencil and tried to visualize the Thorburg stage as she had seen it under the working light. Her mind was racing with ideas. The children's and young people's costumes very easy of course; the ones for the procession more difficult, but scarlet and gold sateen or something shouldn't cost much. Banners? Oh, easily made and painted with gold paint. She could have done them herself, without recourse to the Thorburg workshop.

She went downstairs hours later, looking untidy and dazed.

"What have you been doing?" Delphine muttered, on her way to bed.

"Nothing." But Joan flushed guiltily.

"A secret!" said the child, in tones of high triumph. "Something you oughtn't."

"There's nothing she oughtn't to do," said Anne, putting her books together. "Don't be silly!"

But there was one thing, Joan hadn't done her homework. She carried her milk and biscuits upstairs and worked until eleven o'clock, making herself forget her ballet.

Just when they were getting ready to welcome the travellers home, word came that the Thorburg Ballet Company was going direct to Brussels to fulfil a fortnight's last-minute engagement. The Brussels theatre had been let down by a French ballet company, and there was no reason why the Thorburg should not accept, as the season at the Thorburg Theatre was not to start immediately.

"Pel *will* be pleased!" said Anne. "It's a bonus for her. But oh! it will be nice when they're all home again!"

They all accepted the news philosophically and were so

much occupied that there was little time to think about it. But Timothy Blandford was inconsolable. He began to haunt the house in the evenings, apparently drawing some comfort from the company of Pelagia's brother and sisters.

"If I thought she'd like it I'd fly over to Brussels for a weekend," said the infatuated young man.

"She wouldn't, you know," Delphine said bluntly. "She's having a super time and she doesn't need any of us."

"You nasty, outspoken child! How can you know?"

"I'm afraid she's right," said Anne. "Pel's horribly self-absorbed. I really shouldn't go. She doesn't even want to be reminded of home." She wished that she had the wisdom to say something profound and definite about Pelagia's state, but Timothy would not believe her, and, after all, it was Pelagia's business how she dealt with her admirers. But Anne liked Timothy and it was sad that he was on his way to being badly hurt.

"Oh, well, I won't, then. I suppose the time will pass." And on the Saturday evening, perhaps with some obscure idea of pleasing Pelagia by entertaining her family, he took them all, including Joan, to a much-vaunted American musical.

Joan enjoyed the musical, which displayed perfect stagecraft, but wished it were ballet. Her own ballet was occupying her mind more and more, and she was startled at how real it had become. She could see it so clearly, though suitable music was at first a difficulty.

One day after school she went to the piano in the studio next to her own room, shut the door firmly and began to play.

Anne, half an hour later, heard cascades of sound from above and wondered who on earth could be playing. She climbed the stairs and put her head round the door, and was amazed to see her cousin playing with abandon.

When Anne said tentatively: "Joan!" Joan was so

absorbed, and so utterly lost to her surroundings, that she merely snapped absently: "Leave me alone, do!"

Anne gasped. She had not even known that her cousin could play the piano, and, in a most uncanny way, she had a curious look of Anne's own father when he was lost in something.

She retreated to the window, vaguely recognizing what seemed to be variations on different tunes, particularly a North Country melody, *The Oak and the Ash*. Then, suddenly, the music changed, and – a trifle stumblingly – turned wistful and ceremonial and somehow, Anne thought, Russian.

She could stand it no longer.

"Joan! Why – what are you doing?"

The spell was broken. Her cousin looked round, pushing back her hair.

"I didn't know you were there."

"I spoke to you before."

"Oh, did you? I didn't notice."

"But, Joan, where did you learn to play like that?"

"My mother taught me."

Anne had the groping feeling of being out of her depth, but gradually light began to dawn.

"Your mother! I'd forgotten ... utterly forgotten. When she was young she was a concert pianist."

Joan was still blinking, her defences down.

"I know. It was just that they were a musical family – the Garlands. She didn't really want to be, though she had quite a lot of talent. She met my father when she was on holiday and they married almost at once. She didn't often talk about her career, but we had a good piano and she taught me to play."

"But you never said ... You should have been having lessons and practising."

"When she died so suddenly I thought I'd never want to

play again. Besides, I've had other things to think about. Anyway, music lessons cost money."

Anne still felt a little out of her depth.

"Well, they do, of course. But your mother left some money, didn't she? And even if she hadn't – for a thing like that Father would have said ... But we thought ... Oh, dash it all, you know, we thought you had no artistic talent at all."

"I don't play well. I could never earn my living that way."

"But – but you said you didn't know anything about ballet. You must have known the music, anyway."

"Well, I knew some of it, of course. But Mother didn't like ballet and she seemed rather to despise Delibes and Tchaikovsky. But I don't. I can't. That Delibes record you're always playing, with the drums ..."

"*Sylvia.* Yes, some of it is splendid, though I don't like some of the string parts. But, Joan, you say you don't play well, and yet that sounded like improvising. What was it?"

By now Joan had had time to grow stiff and shy again.

"Well, it was sort of improvising. I was trying to make an arrangement of some North Country tunes: *Bury Fair*, and *The Oak and the Ash*, and the tune they use for the Bacup Coconut Dance. I don't know what it's called."

"Was that the odd one? Modal, is it? Folk?"

"I suppose so. I don't really know anything about it, but I often saw the Bacup dancers."

"And the end part?"

"Oh, that was sort of Russian. Based on that Borodin thing Pelagia's got on the back of one of her records. *From the Russian Steppes*. Or *From the Steppes of Asia*. Something like that."

"But, Joan, why? What's it for?"

"Oh, nothing."

"If you really want it Father could do it. He has done

some composing; I suppose you know? The music for some short Thorburg ballets."

"I didn't know," said Joan, and, when Anne had gone away, she sat there for a few minutes longer, frowning into space. After all, it was pointless labour. Nothing could come of the ballet. It was a secret thing, just to satisfy herself. And yet – a ballet needed dancers. A ballet needed to be seen.

Chapter Twelve

Disappointments and Triumphs

Anne was vaguely puzzled about Joan during the next few days, but, as usual, there was little time for thinking. It was already the beginning of November and things were boiling up into tension and excitement at the Thorburg, now that the time for choosing the dancers for the Christmas Show was drawing near.

Lisa, in fact, was probably the only student in the School to remain calm and untouched.

"You don't know what a relief it is," she said one day, as she walked round Russell Square with Anne and Fernanda. "I'm out of the rat race."

They looked at her in silence and she laughed rather shakily.

"Oh, yes, I do mind in some ways. It seems so strange; rather as though I'm going to die at Christmas."

"*Is* it a rat race?" Anne asked.

"You know it is. During the next week or two you'll all be secretly wanting to scratch each other's eyes out. It's inevitable, but I always hated it. Father hates it, too, but there's nothing he or anyone else can do about it."

"I long to be chosen," Anne said, very seriously, "but if I'm not – well, I shan't do any scratching. I shall just grin and bear it. I agree with you that it's awful, and when I think of Helenka and me that time …"

"Fighting tooth and claw? Yes, it was dreadful, but you couldn't help it."

"I can help it now. I'm nearly fourteen and a – a conscious human being. Not a kid with a violent temper."

"Well, let's forget the Thorburg," Lisa said quickly. "On Saturday I'm going to my aunt's farm near Princes Risborough. By train by myself. Why don't you both come?"

Fernanda said that she was going out with her aunt and Lisa laughed.

"Confess that you don't like the country, you native of Barcelona!"

"Well, not so very much. It is so quiet, and so much mud, and animals smell horrible."

"Pigs, perhaps. Cows and horses smell rather nice, I think. Oh, well, Anne?"

"I'd like to," said Anne, who slightly shared Fernanda's feelings about the country, but who thought that a day away from the ballet atmosphere might, in a strange way, be a relief.

"Why not ask your Joan?"

Anne frowned.

"Joan? Oh, I don't know …"

"She must miss the country a lot."

"I suppose she must. Not that the Chilterns are in the least like the Lancashire moors."

"Still, why not ask her? I'd like to get to know her better. After all, I'm going to her school after Christmas."

Anne was conscious of an unexpected little wave of jealousy, quickly suppressed.

"Oh, then I will if you like. But perhaps she won't come."

But Joan, rather to her surprise, jumped at the invitation. No one knew, except Margaret, just how stifled Joan had sometimes felt in London, even though she was growing to love it.

"Thank you, Anne. I'd like to go. Is it far?"

"Oh, not very. Under forty miles, I think. It's lovely countryside. Beechwoods and the sort of flowers you get on chalk."

"But there won't be any flowers in November, will there?"

"I don't know," said Anne vaguely. "There might; it's been a mild autumn. Or berries, perhaps, and that old man's beard stuff that grows over the hedges like great cobwebs. I don't know the first thing about wild flowers, do you?"

"Oh, yes. We didn't have many near us in Rochdale, but Mother and I were both keen. We used to go to Arnside and Silverdale for the day sometimes, where there are a lot, and over to Ainsdale and Formby. There were all sorts of lovely things near Formby – bee orchids, and wild pansies, and heaps of others. And I have some flower books. I know about the chalk flowers. Milkwort, and rock roses, and helleborines, and wild arum."

"Then you know more than I do. Oh, well, I'll say we'll go. We'll get an early train from Marylebone."

Anne still made Joan feel awkward, but Lisa was a different matter. Lisa seemed to Joan much more ordinary and easier to know, and she had shown such calm common sense over contracting out of ballet.

Though it was November the sun was quite warm and there was no wind. When the train at last left the furthest outposts of London the blazing scarlet and gold of the beechwoods burst on them, and Joan gasped and stared, for she had never seen such trees in her life.

"We're lucky," Lisa said contentedly. "I often miss the autumn colours altogether. I go in October and the trees are still green, and then, a few weeks after, they've been stripped bare by frost or a gale. Aren't they heaven? And those pale yellow hazels ..."

"It's beautiful. But very – very civilized country," said Joan.

"We-ell, it must seem so to you after those bare, wild hills, but really the Chilterns can be very lonely. I've often walked alone when I was staying with my aunt. If you broke your ankle in some of the woods you could easily lie for days. Oh, it's lovely! You should see the Icknield Way, and all the little hamlets with the fascinating names: Summer Heath, Christmas Common, Lacey Green, Whiteleaf, Bledlow, Maidensgrove."

Joan laughed. She felt oddly relaxed and very different from how she had felt since her arrival in London.

"Are they really the names of places? Maidensgrove? I like that!"

"Oh, there are heaps more. Cow Common, Hampdenleaf Wood, Honor End, Fingest, Green Hailey; even Dancers End. I've often wanted to try to put them in a poem. I suppose your northern ones are quite different?"

"Yes, harsher. Wardle and Syke and Naden. We don't go in for anything so pretty as Hampdenleaf. Watergrove is about our best."

"You do love your North Country, don't you?"

Joan looked at Lisa with a shade of defiance.

"Yes. It's real, and the wind blows, and the curlews cry."

"Oh, but this is real, too. There are different kinds of reality, surely? It doesn't mean that because somewhere is beautiful that it's less real than somewhere smoky and ugly. And the Icknield Way is ancient – so very old that you can feel it in your bones."

After the crowding houses of High Wycombe, the train headed towards a valley between the hills, and Joan sat in silence, staring out at the glowing woods and at the warm russet roofs of cottages and farmhouses.

They left the train at Princes Risborough and set off to walk towards the foot of the hills, with Lisa pointing out the great chalk splash of Whiteleaf Cross.

"We might go up there afterwards. My aunt's farm is below Cop Hill. It's a climb, but worth it to get on top.

Goodness! It's hot."

"I thought we'd said goodbye to summer," said Anne, contentedly carrying her coat and feeling with pleasure the sun on her bare arms.

Once they had left the houses behind there was the smell of grass and earth. The newly ploughed fields were grey-white, like corduroy velvet, and here and there a scarlet or blue tractor gave a vivid touch of extra colour to the scene.

Climbing up the steep road that was little more than a lane, Joan exclaimed over the trailing travellers' joy, as Anne had said, just like pale cobwebs in its autumn state of old man's beard; and there were still a few scabious and toadflax in the hedge.

By the time they approached the farm, which was tucked into a small valley under the hills and woods, she had seen knapweed, fumitory, and a few late poppies in the corner of a ploughed field.

Anne, a little amused to be instructed, allowed herself to be told the names of the ones she didn't know.

"But I shall have forgotten again tomorrow. It's not the kind of knowledge I can hold on to."

"She's a complete city person, isn't she, Joan?" said Lisa, laughing. "She's even afraid of cows."

"So I am," said Anne. "Keep me well away from there!"

The farm and its buildings were made of flint, with russet tiled roofs which are so common in the district, and Joan thought that they looked as though they had grown out of the flinty soil just as the blackened stone farmhouses of the northern hills seemed to have done.

They received a warm welcome and almost immediately sat down to a huge lunch. Afterwards Lisa's uncle, Mr Gray, took them for a tour of the farmyard and Anne picked her way daintily, wrinkling her nose a little and keeping a wary look out for large animals.

Lisa's uncle was a small, dark man whose family had

farmed the land for generations, and her aunt – Johann Thorburg's sister – was a small, homely woman, who had met and fallen in love with Lionel Gray when on holiday after an illness.

"We hear that you're giving up dancing," said Mr Gray.

"Yes. I – I decided that that's what I want. I thought about it very carefully."

"Well, best to do what you really want. It's hard on your Dad, but then he only wants your happiness."

"Yes, that's what he says," said Lisa, and was rather silent for some time.

But, a while later, as they neared the top of the hills, she grew light-hearted again. She led the way unerringly into the woods and presently they came out on a grassy hillside, where the valley lay far below. And Joan gasped to see the wide view – the great sweep of the Vale of Aylesbury, with Whiteleaf and Monks Risborough lying directly below.

"It's a pity they've built so many horrid little houses round Princes Risborough, but it's still a grand view," said Lisa, leading the way to a large patch of bare chalk and sitting on the edge of it, with her legs dangling. "Come and sit on the Cross!"

"On the *Cross*? But –"

"I showed it to you from below, remember? You can see the arms down there and the huge base."

"Good gracious!" said Joan, but she didn't sit down. She wandered about on the grass and presently gave a little cry. "Oh, what is it? Can it be a gentian? Look!"

The others came to look at the small purple flower in the short grass.

"Here are more," said Lisa. "I think they are gentians."

"Take some," Anne suggested, but Joan shook her head.

"No. If they're gentians they're quite rare. I wouldn't do it."

"Other people will."

"Mother always told me not to take unusual things. Just examine them and perhaps draw them." Joan groped in her shoulder-bag for a pencil and a piece of paper and, crouching awkwardly, began to draw.

"Gentians in November! Or they might be tiny little bell-flowers. But I'd sooner think they're gentians."

Anne gaped, rather as she had done when she found her cousin playing the piano. As the drawing progressed she could see that it was very good.

"I didn't know that you could draw, Joan."

Joan, without looking up, said, with a return to her brusque manner: "Well, you don't know everything."

Anne laughed.

"No, I see that I don't. I've been an idiot. But don't bite my head off. If you won't tell things ..."

"I know. I love drawing. I wouldn't mind teaching art."

Over her bent head and careful pencil Lisa's and Anne's eyes met, saying clearly to each other that there were certainly things they didn't know about Joan Bradshaw.

Going back down the hill to the farm they were very merry, singing and laughing over small jokes, and Anne was once more amazed, and, in her heart, deeply relieved. For the first time she began to see a hope of making friends with her cousin and, surprisingly, it suddenly seemed almost an attractive prospect. The grim, silent girl, who had arrived at the house in Moone Crescent like a being from another world, was certainly not as she had thought. Music ... improvising ... drawing ...

"I wouldn't have believed she could be like this," thought Anne.

In the early evening they were driven to the station in the Grays' car, and they looked out of the train as the blue shadows deepened over the heavy golden woods, and traces of bonfire smoke drifted across the pale, newly ploughed fields.

"It's a beautiful, beautiful place!" said Joan.

"Better than the North?" Anne asked mischievously and was rewarded with the first really warm and friendly smile she had ever had from her cousin.

"Different. Quite different. But I could love it."

"We'll go again," said Lisa, as they left the train in the coldness of Marylebone Station. "Ugh! It's gone chilly now! It feels like winter after all. We'll go in the Christmas holidays. It'll be lovely then, too. I'll show you the spindleberries and the wayfaring-trees and dogwoods along the Icknield Way, or the clumps of old box trees near Chequers."

"Thank you, that would be lovely," said Joan. "I'll look them all up in one of my books."

Monday found Anne back at the Thorburg and now excitement really ran high. Soon, surely, would come the day of choice? It couldn't be deferred any longer.

Anne worked harder than ever in her ballet classes, and almost everyone else did the same. Helenka, still quiet and withdrawn, seemed to improve in technique with every day that passed and there seemed little doubt that she would get a chance to dance in the Show.

Half-way through the week, news of the proposed programme began to filter round the school. Two new ballets, composed and danced by senior students, were to be put on, and for the boys and girls of the middle part of the School one of last year's short ballets was to be revived. Then it had been done by the Seniors and Anne remembered it well.

It was charming, with simple but telling choreography by Johann Thorburg himself. It was called *Sea Music* and there were plenty of parts: King Neptune himself, mermaids, sea horses – all the under-the-sea denizens. The main roles, apart from Neptune, were those of the two mortals – a boy and a girl – who had strayed into this enchanted world, and the Mer Princess.

"If only – if only I could be in it!" Anne sighed to Lisa.

"There are plenty of parts, in a way, but think how many people there are to choose from. Of course the younger ones have their own ballet. That's surely going to be the Toy Town one they did two years ago, when I was the Big Doll and you were the Teddybear."

"Soon you'll know," said Lisa sympathetically.

Some of the dances from *Sea Music* began to be taught in the classes and by the time that Mr and Mrs Garland and Pelagia flew home from Brussels at the weekend Anne was in a state of nerves, hope alternating with despair.

The travellers were full of stories of their adventures, and it seemed that the Company had had a wonderful success everywhere.

"Oh, Brussels was superb!" cried Pelagia. "I don't think I've ever been so happy and alive before."

"Timothy nearly flew over to see you."

"I'm glad he didn't. I wouldn't have had time ..."

"But he's haunted us. He's missed you terribly."

"Poor old Tim!" Pelagia said absently.

Shortly afterwards the young man himself was on the telephone and Pelagia returned to say: "Well, it's nice to be missed. I'm seeing him tomorrow. But really I think I shall soon have to damp him off a bit."

"Oh, Pel, that would be cruel!" Anne was appalled.

"It wouldn't, just common sense. I did warn him in the first place. I haven't *room* in my life for someone who wants to see me every spare minute."

Mona Garland sought Anne out at bedtime.

"How was everything, Bunch? How is Joan? She seems very quiet still."

"Oh, that was only because you were all talking your heads off. She's been lots better lately. I almost like her, Mother. And you'll never guess ..." She told about Joan's unsuspected talents, and the day in the country.

"Well, that *is* good news! I must talk to her in a day or

two and see about arranging music lessons. And extra art, if she'd like it. How about Delph? She seems just as full of herself as ever."

Anne groaned.

"She is. She's still awful at the Thorburg. And she's convinced that she's going to get a big part in the Junior ballet. The Big Doll, at the very least."

"Oh, are they doing the Toy Town one again? But the Big Doll is the main part."

"I know. So does she. I think it will be that pretty little Gwen Drake in the class above her. She's a very good dancer, by all accounts."

"I'm afraid poor Delph may be in for a shock."

Two days later Anne came flying home. She crashed into the house.

"Oh, Mother! Mother! I've got it! I'm the Girl! The mortal in *Sea Music*. And Colin is the Boy. Isn't it superb? Wonderful! Oh, I'm so happy!"

"Oh, that's splendid!" cried her mother, while Annali and Rosa, who had both rushed to the scene, added their congratulations. "And Helenka?"

"The Mer Princess. It's just as good a part. Oh, fate has turned kind. Oh, isn't it absolutely perfect?"

And Anne tore up two flights of stairs to hurl herself into Joan's room without knocking. Joan, carefully fitting something together on her small table by the window, jumped violently and tried to hide her work.

Anne scarcely noticed.

"Oh, I'm sorry, Joan. I should have knocked. But I've got it! The Girl part in *Sea Music*. Oh, you will come and see me?"

Joan said warmly, looking at her cousin's enraptured face: "Of course I will. I'm so glad, Anne. We'll all come, I suppose. What about Edward and Delph?"

"Oh, Ed's King Neptune. He's all right. Delph got

nothing. I didn't think she would, there are so many of them. I'm afraid she'll be upset, but she'll have heaps of other chances. After all, it's her first term." Then Anne really saw what Joan was trying to conceal.

"*Joan!* What is it? Let me look!"

"No, it's private. Don't look!"

But Anne was bending over the model on the table, her bright hair swinging forward.

"But, Joan, you've made a stage! A set ... Oh, how clever! Just as the real designers do. I've seen their models in exhibitions. But what is it for?" And she crouched over the small, neatly made stage, with its carefully painted wings and backcloth. "Joan, a street! A northern street, is it? Tell me. I must know. I won't be snubbed." A pause. "What is it for?"

"It's not for anything. I've just done it for fun."

"But ..."

"You know you talked about the ballet competition?"

"Yes, of course I did. Only a few went in for it. They've chosen two, both by Seniors."

"Well, I thought I'd try."

"You've – made a ballet?" Anne completely forgot, in her amazement, all thoughts of her own triumph.

Joan was flushed and shy, still trying to protect her creation.

"I don't suppose it's any good. This is the set, and these are the costumes." She waved some coloured drawings under her cousin's nose.

"Children? Boys and girls? I like that one in the yellow dress."

"She's the heroine. She's not really a child. I think she's about sixteen. It doesn't matter. That's the boy who is in love with her. He works in a mill. I've written the story down. It's here."

"But those brilliant ones. Red and gold and white. What are they?"

"The people in the procession. There are lots of Russians and Poles living in the North and they used to have processions on Saints' days and so on. With banners. It's called *The Procession Passes*. It takes place years ago when there were a lot of cotton mills. You see ..."

Anne snatched the story and read it quickly.

"I see. It sounds splendid! So simple, but unusual. And the music?"

"You heard me trying to sort it out. Northern tunes and then a sort of Russian thing for the procession. I couldn't really do it."

"Then you must ask Father tonight. Play them all to him and tell him what you want."

"But why? I don't understand. I won't have anyone else see it."

"You jolly well will! You haven't done it just for yourself. I'm taking it to the Thorburg. Or I shall ask Father to. They need another ballet. Why shouldn't it be this?"

"But, Anne ..."

"No, honestly, I mean it. But now I must fly and wash."

Anne shot off, and Joan stood looking thoughtfully down at her model. A ballet needs to be danced ... to be seen. She sat down on the bed and stared blankly at her Lowry picture.

Chapter Thirteen

Delphine Dances

Delphine arrived home late, in a towering temper. Her curls were wildly untidy, her eyes flashed sparks of green fire, and she flung her case the length of the hall, so that it only narrowly missed Rosa, who was just emerging from the kitchen.

Mona Garland intercepted her youngest child before she had a chance to go upstairs.

"Delph! What a way to arrive home! What's the matter?"

"Matter?" Delphine glared. "Haven't you heard, Mother? I didn't get a part in the Show."

"Well, we didn't really expect you to, your first term. And when you've been behaving so badly, too. Calm down."

"I'll never forgive them! Never! I'll show them – I'll make them sorry!"

Mona Garland put a hand on her arm and drew her into the empty drawing-room.

"I said calm down, and I mean it, Delphine. This is ridiculous behaviour and you know it. If you can't learn to take disappointments quietly you'll never make a dancer."

"I will! I will! I'll be famous in spite of them. Carrie's got a part and that insipid Gwen in the next class. *She's* got the Big Doll. I – I could scratch her eyes out!"

"Delph!" Mona Garland, really shocked by the red-haired virago before her, hardly knew what to say. "If you don't stop it at once you'll go to bed without anything to eat."

"Well, but really, Mother, it *is* an insult. How am I to face them all? I dance quite as well as Gwen."

"I very much doubt it. Gwen has been at the Thorburg for well over a year and she deserves the part. You don't – yet. Next year it may be different. Now go and wash your face and brush your hair and try to behave more sensibly."

Delphine, calmer on the surface at least, obeyed, but the evening meal was an uncomfortable affair, with Edward and Anne reluctant to show their pleasure in their own achievements while Delphine acted the part of a martyr. Joan, lost in her own thoughts, was silent, and Edwin Garland looked in some despair round the table.

Mona Garland and Pelagia went off to the theatre, but Edwin Garland, who was not conducting that evening, retreated to his study. There Anne followed him, having insisted on borrowing Joan's model, drawings and suggested story. Edward went out, Delphine played the record of the music for *Petrushka* and Joan wandered restlessly from the kitchen to the studio and back again.

Eventually Anne emerged and caught her in the hall.

"Father wants to talk to you. He thinks your designs and ideas splendid. Go in, Joan."

Joan entered the study shyly and her uncle put down the designs he had been studying and turned to her slowly.

"So you're a chip off the family block, after all? It's a clever idea. How have you managed it when you've seen so few ballets?"

"I don't know. I'd seen ballet on television and then we were taken to an exhibition of designs for sets and costumes. That's how I knew how to do it."

"It took some creative thought as well," he said dryly. "Now what do you want for music? Anne said you were trying to make an arrangement of North Country tunes."

"Yes, but I couldn't manage it. And I don't know, anyway, if people could dance to them."

"That would be up to the choreographer. Come into the drawing-room and play them to me. Let's see what we can do."

"But I can't play to *you*!" Joan cried in horror.

He gave her a gentle push towards the door.

"Yes, you can. You can't abandon it now."

In the drawing-room Joan sat down at the grand piano and stared at him helplessly.

"It's three tunes. I would like arrangements and perhaps variations of *The Oak and the Ash, Bury Fair* and one of the tunes the Bacup dancers use. *Bury Fair*'s a folk dance, I think. We used to do it in school."

"Well, let me hear them."

At first she was stiff with nerves, but she had a sure touch, though she had not practised for weeks. Edwin Garland, knowing himself half-forgotten, raised his eyebrows in astonishment and settled on the arm of a chair. Presently the three first airs drifted into something that was very different – the alien music for the procession.

In the end Joan stumbled and turned a flushed face.

"That's meant to be something from Borodin. I don't remember it properly, but anything recognizably Russian would do. That would end the ballet, with the heroine dancing off after the procession. She's attracted to the boy leading the procession and forgets her old love."

Edwin Garland fetched a pencil and a manuscript book and returned to her side.

"I've got *The Oak and the Ash* somewhere, and perhaps we can get *Bury Fair*. I'll telephone the English Folk Dance and Song Society. You'll have to let me write that Bacup

one down, or of course the Folk Dance Society may know it. I see exactly what you want and the ballet should run for about twenty to twenty-five minutes, with the children's dances, and then the two lovers and finally the procession and *their* dance. All right. Let's get down to it."

And Joan found herself, for the next two hours, working in close collaboration with her uncle. At the end he said: "Well, I'll take it to Thorburg. I think he will do it, but don't be too disappointed if it falls through after all. It's a wonderful try."

Some days went by and Joan did her best to forget her ballet. As November passed, and with end of term examinations drawing near, she worked harder than she had ever done in her life, determined to show everyone that she was not stupid. But she and Margaret found plenty of time at weekends to continue their exploration of London, and one Saturday afternoon they went to Covent Garden to see *Petrushka, Antigone* and *Les Rendezvous*. Joan was by then very familiar with the music for *Petrushka*, for the record was a favourite with all the Garlands, but she was scarcely prepared for the vivid excitement of the Fair, the milling crowds of dancers and the blaze of colour. The drum notes that carried each scene on to the next were not on the record and came as a surprise, and she sat tense and thrilled as the ballet moved on to the end, with the snow beginning to fall and the spirit of Petrushka appearing on top of the booth.

"I could just see it over again right now!" she said to Margaret. "Couldn't you?"

"Oh, I could!" Margaret cried, for she was beginning to learn a little about ballet and was getting caught up in its fascination. *Petrushka* was not in the least like *The Sleeping Beauty*, but it was really an even more startling experience. *Les Rendezvous* was pleasant, but less moving. Then came *Antigone* and Joan sat with her hands tightly clasped, carried away by the violence and strangeness of the music, and by the intense atmosphere of tragedy.

At the end she said slowly, blinking: "It makes my little ballet seem silly and pointless."

"Are they going to do it?" Margaret knew all about *The Procession Passes* now.

"I don't know, Peigi. I expect not. I've heard no more about it."

But when Joan arrived home her uncle called her into the study.

"Thorburg has just been on the telephone. He's going to put your ballet on as part of the Christmas Show. They'll start rehearsing it on Monday. Thorburg himself is doing the choreography."

Joan stared at him, quite overcome.

"Really to dance it?"

"Yes, I'm very proud of you. Not one of my own children has ever shown this kind of creative urge, and we need designers in the ballet – anyone with ideas. It will make a splendid contrast to the other items on the programme."

So Joan was happier than she would have believed possible when she came to London, and more happy still when Anne came flying home on the Monday afternoon.

"Oh, Joan! I'm in your ballet! One of the senior students is the Girl, but I'm one of the older children. Mr Thorburg has made a lovely little dance for them. Oh, Joan, isn't it fun? Aren't you pleased?"

"I can't believe it," said Joan, and wondered fleetingly what her mother would have thought. Perhaps she wouldn't have approved, since she had taken such pains to keep away from her brother's "ballet world". And yet she would have wanted her only daughter to be happy, and there was a quite startling amount of happiness in the thought that, in the Thorburg workrooms, her designs were taking shape.

A fortnight later she was taken there to see the unfinished backcloth and it was an extraordinary experience to see her design faithfully reproduced on such a large scale. It was the same with the costumes, which were also progressing rapidly. The children's dresses were very simple, but the ones for those in the procession were in vivid orange and red and white, the banners in the same colours.

"Of course they look cheap and garish near to," said the woman in charge of the workroom. "But wait till you see them on the stage."

"You'll have your name in the programme, of course," said Anne, who had escorted her to see the set and costumes. " 'Book, costumes and scenery by Joan Bradshaw. Scenery built in the Thorburg workshop.' Isn't it thrilling?"

Conversation at meal-times seemed almost entirely to be about the different ballets, and poor Delphine was the only one out of things. It really was rather hard on her, but, after a stormy week, she seemed to have grown more reconciled. She spent a surprising amount of time practising in the studio.

"I can't quite understand it," Mona Garland said to Anne. "Why is she working so hard *now*? I'd like to think that she's reformed, but somehow I doubt it. I know my Delphine, and there's a look in her eyes I don't quite like. But I can't get a thing out of her." Then she added: "You seem much happier these days, Bunch. Is everything going well at the Thorburg?"

"There's hardly been time to think, with all the rehearsals on top of ordinary classes and working for end of term exams," Anne confessed. "I still feel dreadfully sad when I remember about Lisa, but I've sort of put that away, to be coped with later. And of course there's still Helenka."

"Are you still not speaking to her?"

"We've never exchanged a word. I feel awful about it, but I don't know what to do. Even though we're both in *Sea Music* we don't speak. What can I do? If I try to make friends now she'll snub me, and I can't bear that."

"You might bring yourself to risk it, I suppose."

"Oh, I can't. I'd feel such a fool and the others would laugh. Perhaps something will turn up."

Delphine's behaviour certainly was rather unusual, for she had never been known to practise long alone. Now, every evening, she shut herself up in the studio for quite a long while. But everyone was too busy to think much about it.

Then there came an evening when Anne, Joan and Delphine were at home alone. It was a cold, sleety night about the middle of December; Mr and Mrs Garland and Pelagia were at the theatre and Edward was out.

Delphine had said, during the meal, that she had a headache, and while Joan and Anne were settling down to their homework, she sighed and said that she thought she'd go to bed.

"Ask Annali to give you an aspirin," Anne said, a trifle absently.

Half an hour later she raised her head, listening.

"What was that? I thought I heard the front door close very quietly."

"I didn't hear anything," said Joan, frowning over a French verb.

"Rosa's gone to the cinema, and Annali wouldn't go out without telling us. I wonder –" And Anne flew away, to return in a couple of minutes, looking startled.

"I must have second sight as well as good ears! I sort of thought that Delph was up to something. She didn't *look* headachy. Come on, Joan, we've got to go after her. There's nothing else to do."

"But – I don't understand." Joan put aside the French grammar and stared at her cousin.

"I found this. It was half-hidden under some books on her table. I was vaguely looking for a note. She's the kind who would leave a note on her pin-cushion – if she had one!"

Joan gaped at the printed handbill. It was headed with the name of a well-known public hall and advertised a ballet competition for young people under fifteen.

"She must have got into the finals," Anne groaned. "I see it all. She was determined to 'show' us, and she heard of this – this affair. Look! A cup for the winner and the whole thing to be televised. We've got to stop her!"

"But why? If she wants to ... Won't she get a taxi? I suppose she'll be safe enough. She always seems able to look after herself."

"Oh, she'll be safe, but she'll find herself out of the Thorburg. Get your coat."

Annali looked startled when Anne burst into the kitchen and said they were going after Delphine.

"She's gone to dance somewhere, and we must stop her if we can. It's on ITV at eight o'clock, Annali. Turn it on and have a look. We'll be OK. 'Bye!" And Anne hauled the still slightly protesting Joan away. The bitter wind caught them as they walked into the Outer Circle and Anne looked wildly for a cruising taxi.

Luck was not with them, however, for it was theatre-time and all the taxis were already engaged. It was ten minutes before they managed to stop one in Baker Street and then every traffic light seemed to be against them.

In the taxi Anne explained a little.

"Parents have an agreement with the Thorburg that ballet students won't appear in public without special permission from Mr Thorburg, and they are very strict about it. They don't really like us appearing in public when we're young. It's not like a stage school, where young people often get parts as a matter of course once they're twelve. Delph ought to know. I'm sure she does know. Or perhaps she's forgotten."

"Oh, I see." Joan looked grave. She could not believe that Delphine, in spite of her wild and silly talk, really wanted to be thrown out of the Thorburg.

But when they reached the hall the competition was just about to start and they were refused permission to go behind to speak to Delphine.

"You're not competitors yourselves? Then I'm afraid I can't allow it. The first dancer is just going on and the show is on television."

"As though we don't know!" Anne moaned. Then tried again. "It's really very important. We must speak to someone."

"I'm sorry. You're too late. You must wait till it's over now."

They retreated a few paces and Anne said: "Mr Thorburg has a television set in his room at the theatre. He might even be watching. What *shall* we do?"

"We'd better buy tickets and go in and see," said Joan.

"Learn the worst? Oh, well, if there's nothing else for it. But there probably aren't any seats left."

However, they managed to get two cheap seats at the side downstairs and shuffled gloomily into them. Anne sat down and stared at the stage, where a buxom girl with bleached hair was making a poor attempt at the Dance of the Sugar Plum Fairy.

"Delph must be mad!" she muttered.

But the next competitor was much better: a pretty girl of about twelve, wearing a pink tutu and dancing rather charmingly, though with perhaps too much awareness of the audience. The audience responded by clapping enthusiastically at the end and she disappeared with a flick of her pink skirts.

"Miss Delphine Garland of the Thorburg Ballet School," said the announcer so loudly and clearly that Anne winced. Oh, idiot! Why mention the Thorburg? Why not choose an assumed name? But then Delphine's whole idea was to impress people; she didn't want to be anonymous.

Delphine looked enchanting: a red-haired elf in a short green tutu. And she began to do a dance that was all too familiar. It was the Big Doll's main dance from the Toy Town ballet.

"Mr Thorburg will have the hide off her!" Anne mumbled.

Delphine had, of course, not yet learned point work, but her dancing was so assured and easy, her conscious glances so pleasing to the audience, that she received applause that seemed to the suffering Anne unending.

"Wretched little show-off! She ought to be in the baby chorus in a pantomime."

"But she *was* good," Joan said fairly. "She'll win that cup. There's not much doubt."

"I'm afraid she will. This one isn't very good." And Anne continued to suffer until the fourth competitor had finished her dance and, after only the briefest of consultations amongst the judges, Delphine Garland was announced the winner of the silver cup.

It was presented to a blushing, smiling Delphine, presumably in view of several hundred thousand viewers all over the country.

"Come on! We've got to nab her as she comes out," Anne said, and they pushed their way towards the exit.

But they had to wait in the bitter cold for some time before Delphine at last appeared, clasping the cup against her green Thorburg coat.

Anne pounced on her and shook her hard; she nearly dropped the cup.

"Delph! We tried to stop you, but it was too late."

Delphine glared.

"I wouldn't have let you stop me. Let me go! I won the cup and I've been on television. You ought to be congratulating me."

"We saw you. You danced quite well, if you hadn't done all that self-conscious smiling, but now you've done it, you complete idiot!"

"I don't see why. I *said* I'd show everyone. *You've* never danced on television. You're just jealous."

"I'm not, my dear child. I'm worried stiff for you." Anne saw a taxi, signalled to it and shoved Delphine into it.

"I don't see why," Delphine said again, very belligerently. "I knew that Mother wouldn't let me, of course, and you'd all have sniffed at the idea. You probably think it was cheap. But I had to do something to – to help my ego …"

"It'll need more help soon. Didn't you remember that it's strictly forbidden for Thorburg students to appear in public without permission?"

In the dim light she saw Delphine's jaw drop.

"No-o. I didn't know. I never thought."

"And to have it announced that you belong to the School and to do that dance that belongs to the Thorburg. Oh, Delph!" And Anne sank down into cross, exhausted silence.

"I don't see why they should be so very cross," Delphine said at last, in a most unusually small voice.

Joan was sorry for her, for she suddenly looked very young and vulnerable.

"Perhaps they won't be, if you explain."

"She'll have some explaining to do all right," said Anne, and they drove the rest of the way in silence.

Chapter Fourteen

The Procession Passes

Delphine's life during the next few days was certainly not easy, and she grew very pale and ethereal-looking. Her horrified family eventually began to feel almost sorry for her, and opinions were divided at the Thorburg School, where a large number of the pupils (not to mention members of the staff) had seen the television programme. A few of the Juniors were openly envious of her public appearance, and of her possession of the cup, but the bulk of the opinion was that Delphine had shown off once too often and had, at the same time, lowered the tone of the School.

"We just don't *do* things like that!" was an oft-repeated remark.

"But I saw her on television," Lisa said slowly, "and she did come over well. She's got personality and looks. Still, Father's furious."

"Nothing to what Father and Mother felt," said Anne gloomily. "Though Mother says it's her own fault. She ought to have found out what Delphine was up to."

The affair had not ended with the television appearance, for the next day two of the London papers carried photographs of Mona Garland's daughter receiving the cup, and a few reporters telephoned or called at the house in Moone Crescent. But these Annali dealt with in no uncertain terms.

Two days later the subdued but still faintly defiant Delphine was called before an awe-inspiring assembly, consisting of Mr Thorburg himself, the headmistress of the School, the principal ballet mistress and others. She emerged in tears, but she had been given another chance.

"They s-say I can stay. I told them that I didn't remember about needing permission and all the rest. And I still think it's an awful fuss. Anyone would think I was a criminal!"

Joan, from her position slightly outside the family and the world of ballet, did, in fact, agree with her that it was a terrible fuss and was quite sorry for poor Delphine. Anyone would have thought that she had done something really wrong, instead of dancing rather charmingly in front of some television cameras, but it was useless to air her views and she remained silent. Anyway, she could see that the affair was outside the dedicated, hard-working life of the Thorburg School, where ten-year-olds were definitely not expected to take part in public competitions.

"Anyhow, if they had thrown me out," said Delphine a few days later, when she had recovered some of her usual aplomb, "I could have gone somewhere else. To the Royal Ballet School, perhaps."

"They wouldn't take the Thorburg's leavings," retorted Edward.

"Then I'd have gone to a stage school. They aren't so fussy and – and *religious* about ballet. And I've still got to face the Christmas Show without a part."

"You've got the cup to console you," said Pelagia unkindly.

But Delphine displayed some dislike of the silver cup,

which was eventually thrust out of sight in the cupboard under the stairs.

"Maybe she'll settle down now," said her mother, not too hopefully.

Then everything else was forgotten but the coming excitements. Breaking up was to be on the morning of 22 December and the Show on the 23rd. After that, of course, would be Christmas, and everyone tried to find time to do shopping. The house was continually rustling with the sound of fancy paper, and parcels were constantly being whisked out of sight.

Sometimes, when she thought of Christmas without her mother, Joan felt very sad, but she was too excited about her ballet to be miserable for long.

The dress rehearsal was held on the afternoon of the 22nd and Joan was not able to be there, because she didn't break up until four o'clock. But it would be all the more exciting to see *The Procession Passes* for the first time on the evening of the Show.

She had done very well at the Scott-Smithson, being top in English and Art and second in History, and the report she brought home was quite glowing.

"A very intelligent worker in most subjects. Shows marked artistic talent. Joan has shown character and determination to do well," went some of the comments.

In spite of the busy excitement both Mr and Mrs Garland found time to read and comment on the report.

"So it seems that we did the right thing when we sent you to the Scott-Smithson," Edwin Garland remarked. "You don't regret it now?"

"Oh, no," Joan said. "I like it. But it wouldn't have been the same without Peigi."

Excitement really boiled up on the 23rd and Anne groaned that she was sure the day would never pass. But time could not hang heavily when there was so much to do, and soon Edward, Anne and their father had to leave for the theatre. Mr Garland was conducting the orchestra for the Show.

Mona Garland, Pelagia, Joan, Delphine and Margaret followed some time later in a taxi. The weather had turned very frosty and London sparkled under a nearly full moon. There seemed to be lighted Christmas trees everywhere and Joan and Margaret were enchanted with everything. They had already seen the great tree in Trafalgar Square and were hoping to join the carollers round it on Christmas Eve.

But as the taxi drew near the Thorburg Theatre Joan began to feel the most unusual pangs of nerves. What if her ballet turned out to be awful, after all? She had heard that a few reporters always attended the Thorburg Show; what if they made fun of *The Procession Passes*? Useless to tell herself that it was only a short ballet for young people. She had learned enough to know that, as nearly as possible, the Show was regarded as a professional thing. Anything less than the best would not do, even for a performance given by students of all ages.

The theatre was brilliantly lit, and parents and friends of the performers were crowding in. Their seats were in the middle of the front row of the Circle and Joan sat staring at the heavy red curtain, trying to visualize what it was like now just behind it. Probably the Seniors, who were dancing first, were warming up. Anne would be in one of the dressing-rooms, with her mascot beside her make-up box.

Anne was, in fact, sharing a large dressing-room with a great many others. She had arrived early and was soon dressed in her Mortal's costume and with her face made up. She was nervously wishing that she had not been so early, and consequently with time to think, when she was startled by a commotion in a corner.

When she could see through the variously dressed and undressed crowd she saw that Helenka was standing by one of the dressing-tables, still in her ordinary clothes and looking pale and wretched. In fact she looked ill, and someone had fetched her a glass of water.

"What's the matter with Helenka?" Anne asked someone, and was told: "Her mother's gone to hospital. Appendicitis. They operated this afternoon, and she's come through it all right, but she's very ill."

"Oh, I'm so sorry!" said Anne.

People were fussing round Helenka.

"Shall we tell Mr Thorburg you can't dance? You look awful."

But then the proud, stiff look came back to Helenka's face.

"Oh, no, thank you. Of course I'll dance. Isn't that the first thing we have to learn? That we go on stage whatever happens? I guess I'll be quite all right." And she began to get ready, making up her face with a steady hand. Gradually everyone drifted away from her, intent on their own costumes and nerves.

Overture and beginners ... Soon the curtain would go up. Several people went off to watch from the wings and Anne was going to follow when she saw that Helenka, alone, was struggling into her Mer Princess costume, a filmy green affair.

It must be awful to have your mother go into hospital just before Christmas. Having to dance, in whatever mood you were in, was a hard lesson to learn.

"Helenka!" she said, very shyly and doubtfully, and Helenka finished pulling the costume over her head and spun round.

"Yes?" She looked startled to see that she was being addressed by Anne Garland.

"Helenka ... I'm so sorry, about your mother."

Helenka hesitated perceptibly and then said quietly: "It – it was rather terrible. She was taken ill so suddenly and we were alone. We live alone. I thought she was dying."

The words "We live alone" were the ones that stood out. Christmas –

Anne spoke rapidly and awkwardly, conscious of the silent, difficult months that lay behind them.

"Helenka, I'm sorry. About everything. I'm sorry you're in trouble at Christmas. Where will you go?"

Helenka swallowed and her proud face quivered.

"I don't know. Stay home alone, I guess. We haven't any friends. I don't really know the other people in the flats."

"But you can't! Not at Christmas! It would be – unthinkable. Can't you stay with someone? Someone here?"

"Most of them are going away," Helenka had made a few friends at the Thorburg, but clearly not close ones. No one had thought of saving her from her awful loneliness.

Anne said quickly: "Look! I don't know how you'd feel about it. Perhaps you'd hate it. But you could come to us. Mother would be glad. We'll put an extra bed – we've got a camp one – in with Delph or with our cousin Joan. Or perhaps Pel would move out and let you sleep with me. If – if you'd like it, that is."

Helenka stared at the girl whom she had ignored so successfully for a whole term. No one would ever know, perhaps, just how frightened she had been at the thought of Christmas spent alone in the London flat. She had told herself that she didn't want to know Anne Garland, but in her heart she had been deeply hurt by the way Anne had passed her on that first day of term. Of course they had been rivals years ago when they were little; of course they had fought and seemed to hate each other. But Helenka had known trouble and deep sorrow since then, and when she came back to the Thorburg School the old events had seemed utterly insignificant.

"You wouldn't want me," she said at last. "You have each other. Such a lot of you. And who is Joan?"

"Our Lancashire cousin. She lives with us. She did the ballet, *The Procession Passes*. Helenka, do come!"

"You'd have to ask your mother."

"Oh, she'll say yes, of course. We'll take you home afterwards to get your things and then you can telephone the hospital to say where you'll be."

"It's – it's very kind."

"I want you to come," said Anne, and helped to fix Helenka's green head-dress.

The Procession Passes was last on the programme. Joan saw her own name with pride and awe. "Book, Décor and Costumes by Joan Bradshaw. English and Russian Airs arranged by Edwin Garland. Choreography by Johann Thorburg." Then followed Joan's own brief précis of the story.

It was astonishing! It was unbelievable! And for a brief moment she saw herself in the train coming South, looking at the article called *The Ballet Family*. Then and for long afterwards she had believed that she would always be on the outside. Now, perhaps, she was outside no longer.

She forgot her own nervousness in her pleasure in watching *Sea Music*. How well Anne was dancing and how carefree she looked, though she had been stiff with nerves before leaving home. The Mer Princess was lovely, too, dancing with a grave and assured style.

"That's Helenka Koronov," Mona Garland murmured. "The girl Anne feels so bad about. She shows great promise."

After the interval and another, rather short Senior ballet came the Junior one, and Delphine sat hunched and sulky, glaring down at Gwen during the Big Doll's dance.

"Next year," she vowed, at the end, "I'll have a part or eat my hat!"

Joan was deeply sorry for her, but now it was almost time

for *The Procession Passes*. Her aunt glanced at her sympathetically.

"How does it feel, Joan?"

"Very strange. I hope people don't laugh."

Then the music that she had planned started and a few moments later the curtains slid apart to show the northern street, with the mill chimneys showing over the grey roofs. Boys and girls were playing some game with skipping-ropes, and then the ropes were flung aside and a ball game followed. Anne – as one of the older children – danced a few steps alone on the outside of the group, and then the Girl was there, watched from a doorway by her young admirer.

The Girl danced very lightly and airily and was joined by her partner. He was clearly in love with her, but the Girl was impatient and presently danced away, while the children surged forward again, this time with hoops. But the procession was coming … They abandoned the hoops and everyone gathered to watch as the procession came slowly and ceremoniously on to the stage, banners held high, brilliant costumes glowing in the suddenly brighter lights.

Joan, who had been holding her lower lip tightly between her teeth, suddenly felt a tear quivering on her lashes. There in front of her was her own ballet: a brief reality. And she was strangely conscious of the pleasure of creation. She had made something. Something that had started in her own mind was down there on the Thorburg stage. On the stage of a real London theatre!

She blinked fiercely as she watched the procession break up and some of the leaders dance. That tall, dark boy was French. Jacques somebody. Anne had talked about him. He had seen the Girl amongst the crowd and suddenly drew her out to dance with him. They whirled and twirled, while the abandoned lover stood watching.

Then the procession slowly reformed, the banners caught the light and the brightly dressed figures were moving off. Slowly, slowly. And the boy was smiling and beckoning. The Girl hesitated, looking about her. Her boyfriend tried to stop her, but she danced away in the rear of the procession.

The children surged forward and began to play again as the curtain fell.

And Joan, more shaken than she would have believed possible, would have liked to go somewhere private to cry her eyes out. It had been a most extraordinary experience.

People about her were clapping and even cheering. Even Delphine was clapping hard, her face no longer sulky. Pelagia leaned forward and grasped her cousin's shoulders.

"Congratulations! It was jolly good! The best, really. How did you think of it? I never could."

"But it wasn't only me. The choreography is the most important thing, and Uncle did the music."

"You thought of it, though, and that set was striking. The costumes, too. You're very clever."

"Yes, she is very clever," said Mona Garland. "It was a great success."

"Oh, Joan, it was marvellous!" Margaret cried. "Oh, can't I tell the others when we go back to school?"

"If you think they'd be interested," said Joan.

She followed the others backstage and Anne emerged from the crowd, with Helenka in tow.

"Mother! Mother! Did you enjoy it? Wasn't Joan's ballet splendid? It got the most applause. Mother, this is Helenka Koronov." And Anne spoke very rapidly. "Her mother's just had an operation for appendicitis and she's all alone. I said that she could come to us for Christmas. That we'd take her to get her things, and – I hope it's all right?"

"Quite all right." And Mona Garland took the pale, dark girl's hand. "Anne did the right thing. How could you stay alone? We'll be very glad to have you, dear."

"Where is this Joan Bradshaw?" asked a voice, and Johann Thorburg himself pushed his way through the crowd. He was a small man with greying hair and an authoritative manner. "Have you got her there?"

Mona Garland thrust her niece forward.

"Here she is, Johann."

"That was a very effective little ballet. We may make it longer some time, with new choreography, and take it into the repertoire. If you have any more ideas as time passes you can let me know."

"It – I think it was an accident, Mr Thorburg."

"Accident? Rubbish! It was good creative thought."

Edwin Garland, Edward, Pelagia and Delphine went off in the car, and Mona Garland, Anne, Joan, Margaret and Helenka went in a taxi to the flat in Bloomsbury Street. Helenka was away only a few minutes and then came back with a small suitcase.

"It's so very kind of you. The flat seems so quiet."

They drove away under the moonlit sky, and Joan sat almost in silence, feeling tired and happy and yet faintly melancholy. It was over – that exciting evening. Perhaps the most exciting one she had ever known.

"But there'll be Christmas!" said Anne, as, having seen Margaret home, they joined the others over milky coffee and sandwiches. "Otherwise I should feel as flat as anything now that the Show's over."

Annali and Rosa put up the extra bed while they ate and Pelagia obligingly offered to move out.

"Oh, I'll put up with Delph. It's a small room, but we'll manage. She sleeps like the dead and won't bother me. Or if she does bother me I'll deal with her easily enough."

And Delphine grinned quite amiably at her eldest sister, then crammed another sandwich into her mouth before she was driven away to bed.

Half an hour later, when Joan was in her dressing-gown

and was standing by the window, with the light off, gazing out into the frosty moonlight, Anne slid into the room.

"Joan! I didn't think you'd be exhausted. Joan, weren't you pleased?"

"Oh, I was! And I loved seeing you in *Sea Music*. And Edward. It was all so exciting!"

"Do you feel that you belong a bit now? You didn't understand us at all at first, and I'm afraid that we – we were just as bad."

"I didn't know anything. Now I know a little, and I do think it's a very fascinating world."

"Oh, it is. The only one … It's after midnight. Christmas Eve!"

"Yes, I know. I'd just remembered when you came in."

"Well, goodnight, Joan."

"Goodnight, Anne." When Anne had slipped away Joan took off her dressing-gown, climbed into bed and lay staring out into the moonlight.

How long … how very long it seemed since that first dreadful evening in London. So much had happened. And, thinking about those crowded, often difficult months, she drifted into sleep.